Everyday Hero

By

Peggy E. Pate-Smith

For author speaking availability information or to purchase books in quantity and/or for special sales, contact the publisher, Timely Tomes Publishing by email at <u>timelytomes@gmail.com</u>

Published by: Timely Tomes Publishing

Cover Design by: Seneca Smith

Library of Congress Control Number:

2016903540

ISBN: 978-0-9826504-4-8
10 9 8 7 6 5 4 3 2 1
1.Self Help 2. Motivational
First Edition

CONTENTS

Dedication

Dedicated to my students, who ultimately became my greatest teachers.

ACKNOWLEDGMENTS

Acknowledgments are important, they remind us that we don't get anywhere without a little help from our family, friends, mentors, and sometimes perfect strangers.

For the purpose of this book, I would especially like to acknowledge my biological children who have grown up to be extremely fun to be around and also have developed a habit of repeating the words of wisdom I gave them when they were growing up. Oddly, those words have been just as valuable repeated to me when I needed them as they were to them when they needed them. I want to send accolades to my husband William, who is definitely a hero for putting up with me on a daily basis, and I want to acknowledge my mother, Mary Lou Pate, who taught me the importance of humor in creating a heroic life.

I also want to acknowledge Dr. Betsy Coe. She is an inspiration to Montessori teachers everywhere, and also introduced me to The Heroic Journey curriculum used in the Montessori Middle School Program. This reflection book was created to enhance that curriculum through a 180 day school year, but could be used by anyone that cares about kids and wants to help them learn how to become an Everyday Hero.

PACKING YOUR BAGS

DAY 1:

A few years ago my family and I spent a month in Europe. Before embarking on this trip, we had to really consider what type of experiences we wanted to have, what kind of resources we had (money, friends, time) and what we needed to bring with us on this journey. Because we wanted to be able to move quickly through the airport and train stations and we didn't want to have to pay extra baggage fees, each person packed what they needed for the month in a small rolling backpack that could be carried or rolled easily.

Starting with these ideas we were able to organize and prepare for an experience that was both positive and life changing. Preparing for life is a lot like preparing for a long journey and the more time you can think about what type of experiences you want to have the better you know how to pack your bags. This way, you will be ready to do what you want to do and not be weighed down by having the wrong things in your backpack.

Reflection: What are some things you would like to experience during this year of your life?

DAY 2:

What does it mean to be a hero? Most people consider a hero to be someone that does something that takes extraordinary courage or that helps someone else in an extraordinary way. A hero is someone that is worthy of being admired. In a story, the hero is usually the protagonist of the story.

When we think about our own story we realize that we have the power to be the hero of our own lives. Heroes are usually everyday people that realize they have an important task to accomplish and step up to do what needs to be done in order to reach their goals.

As you go through this book you will have the opportunity to think about how you can create a life story that you are proud of. You can be your own hero, every day!

Reflection: What are some choices you can make on a daily basis that will help you create a life story that you love and reach goals that you want to accomplish?

DAY 3:

The word "abundance" means to have more than you need. When you stop and think about your life you may be much more abundant than you realize. Taking time to reflect on all that you have, and even have in abundance helps you to realize that you are more prepared for the journey of life than you might first think. This is a list of resources you may have that you can help you to be successful:

1. Time
2. Family
3. Friends
4. Adults that care about you
5. Dreams for the future
6. Talents or skills
7. Nature
8. A sense of humor
9. A positive outlook
10. A willingness to try new things
11. A love of learning
12. Lessons you have already learned
13. People in your life that you admire

Reflection: What is a resource that you are really thankful for? What is a resource you would like to have more of in your life?

DAY 4:

Sometimes it can be intimidating to start a new adventure. You wonder where the path will lead and you find yourself fearful of what you may encounter. Sometimes those fears can keep you from moving forward. One way to overcome your fears is to acknowledge and accept them.

Feel where those emotions are in your body. Does your throat feel tight? That may indicate you are afraid of speaking up. Does your heart seem to be beating faster? Fear can be felt in your body. It is important to recognize those feelings are there so you can consciously let them go. After accepting the reality of those emotions think about what they are telling you. If you are afraid to speak up, think about why and what you might do to change that. If you are afraid to speak in a large group look up strategies for public speaking. Learn new skills so your fears are not so intimidating and you can change them from stumbling blocks to stepping stones.

Reflection: What is a fear someone might have and what would be your advice for helping them overcome that fear?

DAY 5:

Most people have something they are passionate about. It might be a sport, a movie or book, a specific type of food, or a place. It is amazing some of the groups that are dedicated to very specific things that people are passionate about. Your passions and interests can give you a clue about the paths you want to take in your life. Often people will develop a passion when they are young that will last their entire lives. If there is an interest you have that really intrigues you, this is a good time to think about how you might eventually turn your passion into your profession. For instance someone that loves basketball might consider all the careers that might go along with basketball besides just playing, maybe being a sports announcer, or a coach, the more options you are willing to consider the more paths will be open to you when the time comes for you to make a decision about which one to take.

Reflection: What is something you are passionate about? What might be some career options for that passion?

DAY 6:

There is an old proverb that says, "The best way to eat an elephant is one bite at a time." Sometimes the tasks we are facing in life may seem as enormous as trying to eat an elephant but when you break those tasks into smaller steps and keep steadily doing them one at a time you can reach your goal without too much stress.

Reflection: Think about one goal you want to reach this year, what are some small steps you will have to take to reach your goal?

DAY 7:

Some people love group projects, and others would rather work alone and being in groups makes them feel anxious. If you are a "lone wolf" that prefers doing things on your own, think about the benefits of doing a group project so you can enjoy it instead of just enduring the experience.

1. Group projects give you the chance to meet new people.

2. Group projects lessen the work.

3. Group projects give you the opportunity to improve your communication skills.

4. Group projects help you to be more empathetic as you learn to think about things from the perspective of different people.

5. Group projects help you work on time management skills.

Reflection: What is something you enjoy about working on group projects?

DAY 8:

In any new situation, once you have had a few days to adjust to your new environment and meet some new friends things may look a little less intimidating than they did on your first day. That is how it is when you start any journey, in the beginning, there are a lot of questions you may have but as days pass you start to understand more of what your objectives are and how things tend to flow through the day.

It is important to remember that you need to be gentle and compassionate towards yourself and others as you go through your day. Don't get discouraged if you don't know all the answers about what you are supposed to be doing. You have been given a lot of new information, and it can feel overwhelming. Be kind to yourself and realize that learning takes time, by the end of the year most things that seem complicated now will seem very simple. In the meantime look around and see if there is anyone else that also needs help. Is there a way you could find the answers together or find someone that seems to understand the path a little better that could help you?

Reflection: What are some things you have already mastered that you didn't understand when you started this journey?

DAY 9:

Having a positive attitude can make a big difference in your ability to succeed. Taking control of your thoughts instead of allowing your emotions to control them can change everything in your life. If you feel discouraged about too much homework, think instead about how proud you will feel when you are finished. If you are lonely and feeling like no one is reaching out to be your friend, think about the ways you can reach out to be someone else's friend. Make the first move to let them know something you admire about them or would like to learn from them.

It is easy to focus on what you can't do and feel defeated. Break up your fears and think about what you can do. Instead of worrying about how to write a whole essay focus first on writing an outline of what you want to say or writing a few sentences about the topic. Start and you will be surprised at how much more you can do than you first thought!

Reflection: How can a positive attitude help you to be more successful?

DAY 10:

Now that your bags are packed, and you are ready to start your "heroic journey" it is important to remember that no matter what you encounter this year you have resources, talents, and people to help you be successful. Sometimes it can be easy to think you are all alone on a journey. However, if you look around you can see that although you are on a unique path with unique sights to see and experiences to learn from, you are also experiencing this year with traveling companions that are there to help you reach your goals. So with a steady heart and a smile on your face go forth and be bold!

Reflection: What are some resources you are aware of now that you feel will help you during this year?

CHAPTER 1: FORCES THAT GUIDE

DAY 11:

The American scholar Joseph Campbell recognized that in all sorts of areas: drama, storytelling, myths, religious texts, and psychological development there is a common character known as "the hero." This hero goes through very typical stages referred to as the "heroic journey." The hero begins by answering a call to do an activity or go on an adventure. The hero may choose willingly to accept this adventure, or the hero may feel like the adventure is thrust on them and they have no choice.

As you start this year of school, you have either started the journey of the year excited about the opportunity or maybe not so excited because maybe you wanted to be somewhere else. However, the truth is, the journey has begun and what you make of your path is up to you.

Reflection: How do you think attitude plays a part in what an experience will be like for someone?

DAY 12:

Choosing to have a good attitude is a force you can choose on your journey. There are many other forces that might not be something you choose, but something you stumble across simply because it is the nature of the path you are on.

Since moving to Chattanooga, Tennessee, I have started to do more hiking. One thing about hiking is that nature doesn't grow in ways that automatically make for an easy path. That is why there are guidebooks that help hikers know what kind of trail they will be on before they start a trail. Even on the easy trails, there will be certain points where you will hit an obstacle. When you are hiking it doesn't make sense to waste a lot of time being angry at a steep path or frustrated because there is a boulder in a path, you just accept that those type of things will happen, and you adapt to figure out ways to keep moving. As you maneuver through life, you will find things will go easier if you just accept that sometimes things don't go in the ways you want. Adapting and moving on are good strategies to turn negative forces into small bumps on your path instead of boulders that block your way.

Reflection: What are some ways you have been able to keep moving when something became difficult?

DAY 13:

Disappointments can be a negative force that can get you down. It can be very easy to let even a simple disappointment ruin your entire day. So how do you turn a disappointment into a positive? One way is to think about ten positives that have or could come about in spite of the disappointment. For example if you couldn't find the cool shoes you wanted in your size, it might be helpful to just remember how great it is just to be able to have shoes, a lot of people don't. Or maybe you can think about the money you saved because you were able to buy a less expensive pair. Or maybe it gives you an opportunity to save up money for an even better pair on a different day. There are all sorts of ways to look at a disappointment from a different perspective, and soon changing your negatives into positives will become a habit that will make your life seem to go much smoother.

Reflection: What is a way a change in perspective could help soothe the hurt of a recent disappointment?

DAY 14:

Sometimes life just feels overwhelming. You knew a task was going to be difficult, but then it appears even more daunting than you expected. How do you cope when hard turns into almost impossible ones? It may help to remember all the original reasons you chose the path you are taking. Were you looking for a new challenge? Were you hoping for a specific positive outcome? Or maybe you just took that path because it was the only one available.

Going back and looking at the reasons you chose a path can help you decide how to proceed. Is the path you are on still worth your choice? Do you need to reach out to others that can help you navigate your path? Do you need to take a moment and rest so you can get a new burst of energy to complete your path? Be gentle with yourself and acknowledge that you are in a difficult place. Sometimes just admitting to yourself that you are having a rough time can be a positive way to deal with the stress. Remember to focus on the resources you have to help you make it through. What you focus on grows bigger, if you focus on possible solutions, the path will get easier as you go along.

Reflection: What are some positive things you can focus on today?

DAY 15:

A clique is a small group of friends with common interests or shared experiences that are reluctant to let other people join them. Being in a clique can be an experience that feels good or negative. It may feel good to know you have people to talk with on a regular basis, but it may also feel horrible if your friends aren't around and you haven't made any effort to make friends outside of your comfortable clique.

It can be normal to reach out to people you know when you are in a new experience and avoid the awkwardness of reaching out to new people. Normally, self-consciousness is how cliques get started. Having a group of close friends isn't a bad thing, but it can be a limiting thing. If you grow or your interests change and the members of your clique don't change you may feel very lonely even when you are surrounded by familiar friends.

As you work this year on hero status one very important challenge should be reaching out of your comfort zone to become friends with new people. These people may be very different from you, or you may discover you have a lot in common.

Reflection: What are some character traits you can develop to widen your circle of friends?

DAY 16:

It has taken me a long time to appreciate the word game Scrabble. I always became frustrated because I knew the perfect word existed if only there was an open letter for the word I wanted or if there was just one more vowel to complete it.

It made me angry that I didn't have exactly what I needed to create my "perfect word". Lately, I've realized this was so upsetting to me because I was trying to do the same thing in my life; I was always waiting for "the perfect world". The perfect world would happen when everything in my life would work out exactly the way I wanted it to happen.

Occasionally in Scrabble and life, things do line up just perfectly, but usually, you have to play the letters you have and make the best of it. This strategy isn't just in the game of Scrabble; this is also true in the game of LIFE! When I got mad because things weren't perfect, I was losing time, energy, and resources. I finally understood to play the game of Scrabble or life, I needed to be creative and use what I had instead of what I wished I had.

Reflection: Can you think of a time when you or someone you know or read about, used creativity to provide a solution to a problem?

DAY 17:

Many forces in our life are not strictly good or bad; they can be both depending on the situation. This ambiguity is why I think Einstein's idea about time being relative makes so much sense. If you are on vacation and having a lot of fun, extra time can feel great! If you are stuck waiting for someone to pick you up, and you don't have anything to do, extra time can seem very dull. However, if you use that extra time to think about the plot for a new story you want to write, figure out a new game strategy, or think about how you might redecorate your room then the extra time could be useful.

When you think about any force in your life, realize that the way you are observing that force will determine whether you consider it good or bad. At a different point in your path, that same force may feel very different for you.

Reflection: Think about a force in your life besides time that could be considered a neutral force, neither good or bad, just something that impacts your life. Are there any ways you could transform it into a positive force by thinking about it differently?

DAY 18:

When you think about the people in your life, would you say most of them are a positive force? What are some ways you can tell a person is a positive force? This is an important topic to consider. Sometimes we have the friends we do because they have always been our friends in the past or because we have a common interest. It may be a good idea to examine the friendships in our lives. Think about the people you associate with most of the time. When you are with them do you feel good about yourself or do you walk away feeling negative about yourself?

While it is always a good idea to be kind to everyone, it is also important to be kind to yourself. If someone is difficult to be around but you have to be around them, think about ways that you can make your interactions more positive. It may be that you need to be honest with them about how you are feeling. Often we get stuck in a pattern of treating each other in negative ways without ever meaning to hurt someone else's feelings. Your friend may just be stuck and need someone that cares about them to tell them how their attitude or actions are impacting others.

Reflection: What are some ways to cope with being around a person that makes you feel negative?

DAY 19:

I have a good friend named Brad. Brad is the type of person that makes everyone around him feel good about themselves. When you walk away from a conversation with Brad, you always feel like someone really cares about you, like you are doing something right with your life and can do anything you put your mind to doing. Brad isn't blind to your negative qualities; he just chooses to focus on your positive traits, and because that is what he is focused on, that is what grows in his mind and yours.

If you have a difficult time making friends, it may be because you are focused on getting other people to like you instead of just liking them. Everyone wants to know they are appreciated so finding things that you genuinely appreciate about others can be a way to open up a friendship. Acknowledging the people around us when we spot something positive can build a bond that may lead to a lifelong friendship.

Reflection: Think about a time someone made you feel really great about yourself. What did they do that you could also do for others to help them feel great?

DAY 20:

Each of us has the same amount of time in a day so why does it seem that when you look around some people are getting a lot accomplished while others appear to have barely started? What are the forces that move people to reach their goals quickly and what are the forces that seem to hold people back? There is an old fable told by Aesop called, The Tortoise and The Hare.

The fable tells the story of a very fast rabbit that challenges a very slow tortoise to a race. The rabbit is so convinced that he will have plenty of time to beat the tortoise that in the middle of the race the rabbit slows down and takes a nap. The tortoise quietly crawls past the sleeping rabbit and ends up beating him to the finish line.

If you watch people that get done with projects with what seems like a minimum amount of stress, it may be that they have taken a hint from the tortoise. They have set a goal and determined to finish it. They work steadily and don't get distracted by other things. Once finished, they have time to talk, read, play games, or maybe even take a nap!

Reflection: Budgeting time is just like budgeting your money, it helps you to reach your goals quicker. What are some goals right now that you are trying to reach that budgeting your time would help you reach them quicker?

DAY 21:

Do you enjoy people watching? There is a lot to be learned from observing other people and life as it goes on around you. Sometimes we get so wrapped up in our thoughts that spending some time looking around and watching other people can be an excellent way to gain a fresh perspective. Realizing that life can be lived in many different ways can help you realize that it is o.k. to do things differently every once in a while.

Even simple things like eating at a restaurant that serves food from a different culture, going to a sporting event that is different from your favorite type, or listening to music that is new to you can help widen your world and make your life more interesting. It will also help you to be a more tolerant person.

Reflection: How can learning about new things and having new experiences help you develop more compassion and tolerance?

DAY 22:

Have you ever tried to juggle? Juggling just a few things can be relatively easy, but add in a few more and it can become difficult very quickly. It is the same way with life; this is why weekends and summers feel like such a break. When we have fewer things to juggle, we feel more relaxed and less anxious. So how can we keep our cool when things are flying at us from all directions?

The key to juggling is to keep things balanced and evenly spaced out. The key to doing the same thing in real life is to stay organized. Staying organized helps things to feel more manageable. Keeping paperwork in specific places so you can find it when you need it is a small but significant step to help you stay organized. Developing a habit of assigning a "home" for your belongings and taking the extra steps to escort them home, keeps from wasting time later to look for things you have lost. Keeping due dates and events written down and checking them on a daily basis, helps you plan out when you need to work on projects, so you have plenty of time to finish.

Reflection: What is an organization trick that you use to help you manage your time and balance your activities?

DAY 23:

One persuasive technique that advertisers use to get people to buy their products is called, "bandwagon". Bandwagon is an old term from the mid-1800's when Phineas T. Barnum's circus used a large highly decorated wagon to carry their band. Later politicians used decorated bandwagons when they were campaigning for office. When voters decided on a particular candidate, they would make it clear they were jumping on that politician's bandwagon.

Today the term means that you want to do something because everyone you admire around you is doing the same thing. Jumping on the bandwagon could be anything from reading a book everyone else is reading to buying a specific brand of shoes. While most of the time this isn't necessarily a bad thing, it is important for you to think about the consequences of your choice. Is it something you really want to do, and can afford to do, or are you just doing it because everyone else is?

Reflection: Think about a time you wanted to "jump on a bandwagon" and do something because everyone else was doing it. Were you happy with your choice?

DAY 24:

When Joseph Campbell wrote about heroes, he determined that a hero receives a call to do something meaningful. As you go through life, you may find that you receive a calling to do many different things. Each calling can lead to a different path. The hero knows that each journey offers something new to learn, they aren't traveling their road just to take an achievement test, they are traveling the path to learn skills that will help them on even greater adventures later in life.

It is because you are on your unique journey that it is important not to take shortcuts. It may seem easy to copy someone's homework and get it turned in on time, but if you don't understand the concepts the only person you are cheating is yourself. Most teachers would rather have you honestly come to them and ask for help and an extension if you need it then have you turn in work that is on time but not your own. Teachers want you to succeed, not just on homework but in life.

Reflections: What does the expression, "Your learning is yours" mean to you?

DAY 25:

In the movie Star Wars, Luke Skywalker meets some unlikely but loveable allies including two robots. Just like Luke Skywalker you never know who might be around you that might be able to help you on your journey. Unexpected help is the reason it is important to keep an open mind about the people you meet and interact with on a daily basis. In the Aesop's fable The Lion and The Mouse, the lion saved the mouse's life never realizing that soon the mouse would return the favor and save the lion's life.

Reflection: Who are some other unlikely allies in stories you have read or movies you have seen?

DAY 26:

The word hero may conjure up many different images. It may make you think of someone that rushes towards danger when everyone else is running away, or it may make you think of someone that is dealing with a severe personal battle with a positive attitude. It might even cause you to remember someone that you admire and want to emulate. Whatever your concept of a hero, the important thing to remember is that every hero that has ever walked on the earth has just been an ordinary person. People aren't born heroes; it comes through the choices they make in their lives.

Reflection: What are some choices that you think heroes might make that make their lives look different?

DAY 27:

In a perfect world, every child that is born would have perfect parents and families that love and nurture them. Unfortunately, this isn't a perfect world and sometimes if a parent didn't have a great example of how to be a good parent, they may not know how to interact in a positive way with their own children. In many situations, they may not be able to be there for their kids in a way that is helpful.

If you are in a family that doesn't look like the perfect family portrait, don't despair, you may not have control over your family, but you do have choices. You can choose to do life differently when you start your own family. You can elect to respond in a way that is healthy and safe for you. If you need help, you can talk to a school counselor or someone else you trust. What someone else does can impact you, but it doesn't have to reflect you. You have the ability to choose your own standards for your life and allow people to know you are a person of good character that has an inner moral compass that makes positive choices.

Reflection: What are some positive things you would like to do when you have kids that may be alike or different from what your family does?

DAY 28:

Emotions can be internal forces that whip you around like a one person roller coaster. While the rest of the world is moving on you might be feeling tossed about by emotions that seem to overwhelm you. So what are some ways to deal with feeling happy one moment and utterly depressed the next?

Realize that your body is growing right now, and part of that growth has to do with hormones that impact your emotional well-being. Stopping this emotional roller coaster may not be entirely possible, but there are some strategies you can use to help you cope with them. One of those strategies is to realize that what you are thinking about most of the time is going to impact your emotions. If you are listening to negative news stories or around people that are highly critical it is going to be difficult to stay positive. Being proactive in searching for the good in life is a sure bet to help you slow down your personal emotional roller coaster.

Reflection: When you think positive thoughts you become more positive. What are some ways you can actively seek positive thoughts?

DAY 29:

When you are feeling physically ill one of the first things a doctor will ask you is, "Where does it hurt?" To slow down an emotional roller coaster, take the time to diagnose the emotion you are feeling. This diagnosis works for both positive and negative feelings. Take a moment and think, "How am I feeling, and where in my body do I feel that emotion?" You may feel sadness in the middle of your chest; maybe fear is in your arms. It may seem weird, but when you slow down enough, you can pinpoint where you feel your emotions in your body. Naming and claiming those feelings, helps you to not only get past and let go of them but also keeps you from taking them out on other people. When you realize your emotions are your own responsibility, you also have the choice to make positive decisions about how to work through those emotions.

Think about any negative feelings you might have in the same way you might think of a GPS in your car, an emotion that doesn't feel good to you is telling you that you need to recalculate your life and do something different. This change may be as simple as making new choices, or it may be more involved like getting help from a mentor or a professional. Taking care of your emotional health is just as important as taking care of your physical health because often when you feel overly stressed or upset, it starts to make you feel physically ill also.

Reflection: What are some ways that naming and claiming your emotions might help you to have an easier journey through life?

DAY 30:

When you think about stories you love, the reason for your attraction to them may be due to the characters in the book. The author has made the characters seem so real that they can come alive in your imagination. The protagonist in any story usually has people or things around them that you could easily identify as the allies or ogres for the protagonist. It is the act of overcoming the ogres in their lives that helps a character come across as endearing.

An ogre may not be an actual person, it could be a character trait or an area in your life that you seem to be battling with, an example might be working through a difficult math concept or dealing with shyness. Making friends with your ogres or figuring out how to cope with them in a positive way are the steps you take towards maturity. When you look back after a particularly long or difficult experience in your life, it is the lessons you learn from dealing with your ogres that may be the most valuable to you. When you encounter an ogre in your life, try finding ways to be thankful. It sounds counterintuitive, but gratitude for the ogre lessens the negative power and fear it is causing in your life. Seeing the benefits of the ogres in your life helps you to overcome them and turn them into allies.

Reflection: Think about an ogre that might be in someone's life, what might be some specific lessons or benefits of dealing with that struggle?

DAY 31:

Usually life is easier if we make it a habit to assume "positive intent". This means when there is a situation when we need to judge someone's actions, it is a good idea to try and think about all the possible positive reasons a person might have made the choice or decision they made. Their choice may have come from a place of innocence in not knowing all the facts or understanding a situation, it may have come from misunderstanding the facts, it may have come because they were tired, hungry, angry or sad. Taking time to assume "positive intent" instead of jumping to conclusions can really help you to develop the reputation of being a more balanced person that makes good decisions.

When you speak to others, it is wise to "hold your tongue" and be slow to accuse or come across harshly. Instead of being aggravated and exclaiming, "Why would they have done that!" slow down and think seriously, "Why would they have done that?" Really thinking about that question can help you figure out if there might have been a positive intent that just twisted for some reason and caused a problem.

Reflection: Can you think of a time when you had a positive intent but someone else took your words or actions in a negative way? How did that make you feel? What could have been done differently that would have made the situation better?

DAY 32:

One of the qualities people often admire in a hero is the quality of being a protector. It can feel really good to think about someone taking care of you and protecting you. It can also feel good to be someone that other people look up to as being a protector, as with every other area of life though there should be balance. In reality there will be days that other people help you, and days when you help other people. Maria Montessori said, "Never help a child with a task at which he feels he can succeed." She knew that it was important for each individual to carry their own weight and learn their own lessons in order to feel accomplished within themselves.

You have the right to make decisions for your life, and the choices you make will either widen the way for you or narrow your paths. When you are making decisions that enable you to learn new skills and take on new responsibilities you are automatically being your own protector and hero. When you rely on other people to always do things for you, it is a choice to narrow your life path. While other people might enjoy doing things for you, sometimes it is an unfair emotional or physical burden to put on them and it limits your own abilities and skills.

Reflection: Think about a household job that you don't currently do that you could easily learn to accomplish, maybe doing laundry or making simple meals. How would choosing to do this on your own be helpful to your family or to yourself?

DAY 33:

Money, it can definitely feel like an ally or an ogre. If you are good at managing your money it can help you reach your goals, if you are not good at managing your money it can keep you feeling discouraged. A lot of people feel like they don't really understand money or how to manage it wisely.

This is a great time of your life to start looking at money as a tool. When people say they would like to have more money what they usually mean is they want things in their life that they can exchange their money for on any given day. They may want a physical object such as a new video game, or they may want an experience like going to a concert or out to a movie with friends, or they may want an emotional feeling like security to know they will have money for a rainy day. When you strip money of immediate emotional attachments, it is a lot easier to make good decisions about how to use it. One way to do that is to think of money on a scale of one to ten. When you look at the different ways you can spend money think about which things make you feel good on a scale of one to ten. Detaching like this helps you to make a budget of how to spend your money so you are getting the most emotional bang for your buck! If you love the idea of a concert but just like the idea of new shoes you might want to wait on buying the shoes and save up for a concert.

Reflection: What are your favorite ways to spend money? Does thinking about money as a tool change the way you feel about it?

DAY 34:

In Greek mythology, Mentor was the son of Heracles and Alcmene. In his old age Mentor was a friend of Odysseus. When Odysseus left for the Trojan War, he put Mentor in charge of his son Telemachus, In this role Mentor acted as a guide and wise advisor to the boy.

Today when we talk about mentors we usually mean someone we feel comfortable talking with and know that the advice they give us will be both wise and come from a place of experience. A mentor is different from a friend because usually they are older than we are and have more experience in whatever area we are needing help with. Choosing a good mentor may take a little bit of thought about what you are wanting a mentor to help you with.

Do you need someone to talk about relationships with, or school work, or possible future jobs? You might get lucky and find someone that is able to guide you in all these areas or you may discover that having several mentors for different areas of your life might be helpful. Once you realize the advantages of having a mentor, you will want one for the rest of your life. It feels really good to have someone that is a little bit outside of your life so you can get an outside perspective. It also feels great to find someone who is willing to invest their time and energy into helping you make good decisions in your life.

Reflection: What do you think are some possible advantages of having a mentor?

DAY 35:

Now that you know a little bit more about why having a mentor could be helpful, how do you find someone to mentor you? The best way is to start looking around at the people you already know. Think about people that you admire for some reason. Who are the people that are already living the type of life you would like to live? Who are the adults around you that other adults seem to trust and enjoy being around? Who is someone that you would like to have in your life for a long time and would enjoy spending time with?

A good mentor is someone you can talk to in person or by letter or text on a regular basis. Building up a relationship with your mentor is crucial to helping you get the most out of the experience, and the main responsibility for putting energy into that relationship belongs to you. Most mentors are not going to bug you in order to give you advice, you have to reach out first and let them know that you really mean it when you say you want to know what they have learned about life.

Reflection: Once you find a mentor what are some ways you can reach out to them to let them know you appreciate them investing time in your life?

DAY 36:

Along with having a mentor it is also a good idea to be the type of person that someone else would like to have as a mentor. When you are learning a new skill think about how you would go about teaching that skill to someone else. In this way you are not only making your learning yours but you are preparing for a time when you can share the things you learn. Keeping this mindset helps you to enjoy school and life when things get boring. Find ways to make the things you are learning more interesting. Read more than you have to, research further about a topic. If you can find a way to make something more interesting to you personally, it is more likely that you can find a way to make it interesting for someone that you might be mentoring in the future.

Reflection: Passing along a skill you have learned is a lot of fun. What is something you have already taught to someone else or feel like you might could teach someone in the future?

DAY 37:

Having a physical mentor in your life is great, but you are not limited to just having mentors that are physically in your life. Through reading or watching movies you can learn about the lives of people worth emulating. Since I'm very interested in being a person that pursues peace I love reading books about people that have made peace the focus of their lives. War and violence get a lot of media time, but there are a lot of people that have worked to make the world a better place through peaceful means.

Learning about historic movements like The Velvet Revolution, a peaceful takeover of the communist government in 1989: or Gandhi's March to the Sea, or The Glorious Revolution of 1688: give a wider view of how conflict can be handled. To learn about those topics I've had to do my own research and that has led to a greater understanding of a type of heroism that takes a real strength of character and a willingness to try something different.

Reflection: Who are some people or what are some topics that you would be interested in researching on your own to learn more about in order to enhance your life?

DAY 38:

One of the people I look to as a hero is a woman that went by the name Peace Pilgrim. From 1953 to 1981 Peace Pilgrim walked more than 25,000 miles on a personal pilgrimage for peace. She did this without a crew of people following behind her in a car or corporate sponsorship. She just walked, and talked about peace to anyone she met. I doubt that I'm going to sell all my belongings and start walking across America, but in my own way I do what I can to pursue peace. When you look for people to emulate it is important to remember that you don't have to do everything they did in order to gain from their lives. Take what seems reasonable for you to do and find ways to incorporate their wisdom in a way that makes sense to you.

Reflection: A hero is someone you may admire or want to emulate, but it is important to remember that your life is your own and you have to think through choices realizing there may be parts of your hero's life that are not what you want for your own life. How can you seek balance in looking at another person's life so you don't become disappointed if you can't do everything they do?

DAY 39:

Have you ever had someone in your life that you really admired only to find out later that they did something that you considered really awful? In life it is always a good idea to approach everything with a sense of balance, even heroes! Take what you need to learn from their lives and leave the rest, remembering that heroes are just ordinary people that respond in extraordinary ways in some areas of their lives. It isn't fair to put them on a pedestal so you feel like you can't live up to them, or to be crushed if you find out they didn't make good choices in other areas of their lives.

Reflection: How can you seek balance in looking at your hero's life so you don't become disappointed if they do something that falls short of your expectations?

DAY 40:

Occasionally you are going to meet people that are the very antithesis (that's a fancy word for opposite) of what you are like and what you believe. In those moments there are several ways you can respond including ignoring them, walking away, being obviously obnoxious to them, or you might take it as an opportunity to be a cultural anthropologist and learn what makes them believe the things they do.

I once met a young man that was absolutely my complete opposite, but I walked away from our conversation feeling very blessed to have met him. He didn't change my mind about anything I believed, but I had approached the conversation valuing his inherit worth as a living being and having that attitude opened up a moment in time that I will never forget. My open attitude allowed him the freedom to be very honest about some deep pain he had experienced in his life. Listening to him without judgement it was easy to understand why we had responded to our life experiences very differently. While we had responded differently we also had a lot in common, we both had people in our lives we loved, we both had things we were passionate about, and we both had things we were fearful about. It was in looking for those commonalities that I realized we were more alike than different.

Reflection: Seeing immediate differences between you and another person can cause you to put up a barrier if you let it. What are some things you can look for when you meet someone to get past the barriers to find things you have in common?

DAY 41:

Tolerance. How does it help make a hero's life easier? Tolerance helps us to define our beliefs while honoring the right of other people the same freedom to have a belief that may be different. Tolerance doesn't mean you have to agree with their opinion or behavior; it means you have the ability to respond to them with grace. In time, you may find that you still don't agree with them, or you may discover that one of you may have changed how you feel. There is a freedom in finding you don't always have to believe the same things, with more life experiences and understanding, opinions and lives often change. Approaching the people around you with tolerance and grace creates a space that allows you to change your mind if you need to later, and also allows others the same option in how they respond to you.

Reflection: What are some ways you could incorporate more tolerance in your life?

DAY 42:

Jeremy Gilley was an actor that played some pretty unimportant roles in some very cheesy movies. Maybe it was because he was dyslexic and looked at the world differently, but he decided to move in a different direction in his life and instead of being a movie actor he decided to try his hand at being a director. His first big project was a movie that not only made the world a better place but also put a new holiday on the calendar!

Jeremy's documentary, *Peace One Day* told the story of how he convinced the United Nations to celebrate September 21st every year as the official Day of Peace, a global day of cease fire and non-violence. Creating a special day on the calendar has caused people all over the world to rethink options for solving conflict.

Reflection: Jeremy took something in his life that he wanted to do (being involved with films) but wasn't working and found a different way to accomplish the same goal while making a difference in the world. Is there something you would like to do that approaching it from a different angle might help you reach success?

DAY 43:

The Sound of a Wild Snail Eating is a book by Elizabeth Tova Bailey sharing the lessons she learned from the snail living in a terrarium next to her bed. Elizabeth had a very chronic, debilitating illness that left her sapped of any energy or ability to do anything but watch as the snail moved slowly through its days.

In Elizabeth's situation it might have been easy for her to feel like she didn't have any choices, but Elizabeth saw things differently. She realized she did have the choice to be curious about the life of the snail. Elizabeth would probably agree with the proverb, "Curiosity is the cure for boredom. There is no cure for curiosity."

Reflection: What are some things that you are curious about? How can curiosity make your life more interesting?

DAY 44:

When you think about the road ahead you will be able to choose from a plethora (that's a fancy word for a lot) of options. You get to make all sorts of choices about the type of person you want to be, the lifestyle you wish to live, the kinds of activities you choose to pursue, and the kinds of things you desire to study. When you were little someone may have said to you, "You can be anything you want to be!" As you get older that general concept may narrow as you discover you don't have the talent or abilities to do something you wanted to do, but the sentiment isn't a bad one, just one that needs to be balanced. Think more about it as an idea of lifestyle rather than a specific path that only leads to one destination. Think about the type of lifestyles you would find interesting. Start looking into what it would take to get you to that way of life, for instance if you want to travel, you may think about being an airplane pilot or being a writer for a travel magazine, maybe working for a company that does business internationally. By thinking more about lifestyle you have more options to choose from.

Reflection: Think about various lifestyles that are possible for you, what are some that really appeal to you. Does the idea of living in the country feel freeing and blissful or dull and uninspiring? Does the idea of life in a city feel exhilarating or overwhelming? Choosing the type of lifestyle you want to lead can help you better decide your future paths.

DAY 45:

Humor is a tremendous force to call on when you need a useful ally for the journey. Studies have shown that even just smiling for a few minutes can help lift your mood. It can even be helpful to memorize a few favorite jokes to use when you can see that someone else is having a bad day. Reading joke books or humorous stories can help you develop an inner strength that can guide you through rough days.

Reflection: Think about a great joke someone told you or something funny that happened recently. Did even just thinking about it bring a smile to your face?

STRONG STRUCTURES

DAY 46:

Structures are all around us, but we rarely think about them. Like air, we just accept that they are there and rarely consider what they mean in our lives unless there is a problem. Having lived in "tornado alley" for a long period of my life, I now realize how important it is to have a physical structure that you feel safe in, a structure you can count on during stormy times.

It's also important to have structures that work for you and are strong in a non-physical sense. Your time schedule, the relationships that are important to you, the ways you seek clarity and inner meaning, these are all part of the structures that guide your life.

Reflection: Think about the structures in your life. If one or more of those structures were not strong what would you do to strengthen them? What structures are a part of your life that could keep you going even if other structures fell?

DAY 47:

When thinking about what makes a structure stable, what things come to mind? If it is a physical structure, you want it to be able to hold up no matter what the weather does, with a non-physical structure you want to know that it will be there for you when you need it.

A time schedule is a non-physical structure that only works if you follow it. If you plan to work on your homework at a specific time, make sure you have allowed enough uninterrupted time to do what you need to do. Playing video games in between math problems does not make for a strong structure of your time. It feels like you don't have enough time to get work done if you are trying to multi-task and indulge in leisure activities while also doing homework. If you know you are going to need a break then plan for it. Work for an hour then give yourself a specific amount of time to take a break before going back to work. That way you don't feel like all you are doing is work, but you get all your work accomplished.

Reflection: Creating a time schedule can be a structure you put into place that helps you to get more accomplished. How do you figure out how much time you need to use for each activity to make sure you are using your time wisely?

DAY 48:

Life events that are the most stressful like moving or starting a new school or grade are stressful because you are having to create so many new structures in your life. You are finding a new "normal" by finding what new structures work for you.

Those times of transition can be both good and bad. You have an opportunity to see what did and didn't work in your past and create a positive new structure for your future. Taking the time to reflect on your structures gives you a proactive way to choose new opportunities in your life.

If you felt like a structure didn't work in the past, you can think about what the issues were. It is important to focus on the small things you can change that will have a big impact or improvement on the future. This principle works whether you are organizing your locker or putting together a new schedule for your day. When you try to change too many things too quickly you can become frustrated and overwhelmed with the changes. Choosing smaller things that can be easily changed but still make a positive change will open the door to make other positive changes on a manageable scale.

Reflection: What are some small, manageable things that someone could change that might make their lives easier? An example might be picking out your clothes the night before to make getting dressed in the morning easier.

DAY 49:

Sometimes you have to deal with structures that don't seem to make sense, and you have no control over. Kind of like being stuck in a traffic jam, you feel like you are at the mercy of something you didn't create, and have no power to change. What you can do is choose your attitude about the situation. When things feel stuck or ridiculous it doesn't make your life any easier to be upset about them. Like a boulder in the path when your hiking, you just have to figure out how to deal with the issue at hand and move on.

Reflection: When you are in a system that isn't your making and out of your control, what are some ways you can get through them without getting upset?

DAY 50:

One of the greatest resources you have in creating a structure that works for you is to use your imagination. Try to really imagine what it would be like to use the new structure you want to create. If you would like to create a new morning routine, think through each step. Really try to see and hear what things you would do to help that structure work for you. If you are creating a new workspace, imagine where would the best place to put your books or your pens, where would extra paper go? Do you have a to-do list? A place for trash? If you try to imagine yourself working in that space does it seem comfortable and easy to work in?

Realize that what works for you is unique and how you feel about something really makes a difference in whether or not a structure will benefit you. For example, I don't work at a desk. I sit in the middle of my bed with a lap desk, my computer on the lap desk, and books that I use as resources surrounding me. Most people wouldn't like that type of workspace but for me it works. Remember that just like you, your structures will be unique. They need to be set up in a way that you are comfortable with and help you to be successful.

Reflection: Think about a new structure you would like to implement in your life, what are some things you could imagine about that structure?

DAY 51:

Sometimes you don't have enough experience to even imagine what would make a successful structure. When you are in that situation, it may help to look around and see if you can find examples or people that are doing what you want to do and see how you can adapt their success to fit your life.

You can get ideas from many different sources to help you plan a successful structure for anything from how to set up a study time, how to manage your money, to how to arrange your locker. If something looks interesting, make a note of it and after looking at many different sources choose the ones that seem like they would work for you. Ask for advice, most of the time people are flattered that you noticed they are doing something well and are willing to share what works for them.

Reflection: Think about someone you know that seems to have a successful way of completing a task. What appears to be working for them to make the job easier, and what things could you ask about to help your structures work better?

DAY 52:

If you peer into the lives of different people, you will discover that everyone has a unique way to structure their lives. Their lives can vary from what a family unit looks like, the foods they like to eat, their forms of entertainment, the ways they show or don't show respect, even the way they decorate. All these different attributes go back to structure.

When I think about the structure of my family today, I can see that it is very different from the family I grew up in for a lot of reasons. As you are growing up, you may come into contact with families that do things very differently from your family. Sometimes you may find things you like and want to do when you have your own family someday. The family I grew up in didn't collect art, but one of my friends had a dad that was an artist so walking into her home was like walking into an art gallery. I loved that and when I had my own home it wasn't long before I started collecting art. I didn't do everything her family did; I just chose one thing I liked and made that a part of my life.

Reflection: What is one thing you think would be interesting or good to incorporate into your life that you have seen in someone else's life?

DAY 53:

There is an old saying that states, "Don't judge another person until you have walked a mile in their shoes or spent a day in their life." There are so many things that are difficult to understand until you know where someone is coming from and what struggles they have in their lives. Having compassion starts with understanding that someone else's life may be very different, and each path offers different opportunities and different problems.

We can change some structures in our lives, other structures we can't change, or at least they can't be changed by us. There are a lot of factors that go into the amount of money a family has, or the way they relate to each other. When you start to judge someone's attitude or action not only is it important to attribute positive intent, it is also important to think about what factors they might not have any control over and how that might impact how they feel about the world around them.

Reflection: Have you ever had your opinion about someone change after you got to know them better or understood more about the structure of their life?

DAY 54:

Sometimes it can feel like the people around you are only focused on themselves and don't care about you or about the things that concern you. When you are in that situation, it often seems easier to stop caring about others too. It may feel like you are all alone and lost in the world.

This feeling of loneliness can be an alert to stop and think about your part of the equation. What things have you done to let other people know that you care about them? Have you remembered their concerns and asked how that situation was going? Have you reached out to ask questions about their life? As long as you are not coming across as nosey, people appreciate that you remembered something they have said and genuinely care about them. In other words, sometimes they need a model of caring to remember to ask you how you are doing. It is true that people don't care about what you know until they know how much you care.

So it may be that they need to be heard by you before they can hear you. They need to feel seen by you before they start seeing you. When we stop focusing on ourselves and instead focus on others, it paradoxically allows them the freedom to focus on someone other than themselves.

Reflection: What type of things do you do daily to let the people around you know that you care about them?

DAY 55:

What if the people around you still don't seem to notice you, even if you are modeling the way you want to be treated? At least you learned a little more about someone different from you, if you have given it a genuine effort, it may just be that the person you are trying to reach out to isn't emotionally ready to be your friend, this is their loss, not yours. Keep reaching out to others until you find the friend that can give and take in a healthy way.

Reflection: If we are the type of friend that we want to find in others, we will eventually create lasting friendships. Think about the kind of friend you would like to have, what are the ways you can be that kind of friend to the people around you?

DAY 56:

Structure in our lives is a gift we give to ourselves to help things happen in a smoother, more organized manner. Within that structure, there also needs to be time to relax. Time to reflect. Time to play.

At one time many people determined success through a sign of outward manifestation. How big a house they lived in or what type of car they drove. However, times are changing, and many people realize that material objects are not a great way to judge success. People are starting to look around and think about what attributes bring a meaningful life of wholeness. For some, it may be the relationships they have with others. For some, it is reaching out to help the world in some way. Others are deciding to buy less stuff in order to have less debt and be able to pursue more of their personal interests and friendships instead of working all the time to maintain a big house or expensive car. They are thinking more about living simply in order to simply live.

Reflection: What does success mean to you? What are some ways you determine that you are successful in life? How do you think changing the benchmarks of "success" might change the world?

DAY 57:

Abraham Lincoln is quoted as saying, "The best way to destroy an enemy is to make him a friend."

Hopefully you don't have many or any enemies, but if you do have a person in your life that isn't pleasant for you to deal with, Abe's advice may come in handy for you. Instead of considering that person an enemy, start thinking of them as a friend that you just haven't gotten to know very well. When you think of them, try to consider what things might change the relationship from intolerable to friendly. Is there anything you can personally do that would be helpful?

Start looking for positives in that person. For example instead of thinking of them as bossy maybe say to yourself, "They just enjoy leadership positions." Instead of thinking of them as constantly grumpy consider that they may have a lot of stress or might not be getting a lot of sleep at night. Changing your thinking from the negatives to the positive opens a door of clarity allowing you to see that person from a different perspective. How you think about them will change your attitude towards them, which will also change the way you interact with them. They may still be difficult to deal with, but their negative behavior is not going to weigh down your mind or your life as much. Thinking of them as a friend instead of an enemy starts changing the dynamics of your relationship.

Reflection: Think about a relationship you would like to improve. How do you think the relationship might change if you change your attitude and thoughts about it?

DAY 58:

When considering the structure of your life one important factor to consider is your learning style. If you are a kinesthetic person, you need time in your life that allows for plenty of movement, a naturalistic learner needs time to be in nature on a regular basis. Paying attention to your natural inclinations can help you design structures that are the most beneficial for you.

Reflection: Think about your learning style, what are some attributes you can add to your daily life that will help you to be more productive?

DAY 59:

Diversifying our relationships is a big part of creating a stable structure for our lives. We need people that are different from us in many different ways to give us insight into how to do things in ways we might not have thought of from our backgrounds. Being able to call on people from a variety of backgrounds helps to widen our view of the world.

So how do you cultivate relationships with people that are different from you? Start by giving a compliment about something you admire about someone, ask for their advice, or ask a question to gain a different perspective. Regardless of how you do it, cultivating relationships with people that are different from you will help you to be a more well-rounded person. Learning from and listening to others is essential to giving your life a stronger structure.

Reflection: Think about your friends, are they very similar? What might be some benefits to making friends with people that are different from you?

DAY 60:

"By liberating women from household work and helping to abolish professions such as domestic service, the washing machine and other household goods completely revolutionized the structure of society."
Ha-Joon Chang

It is interesting to think about structures that have changed over the years. Things that seemed unchangeable slowly fade away, and sometimes without much notice. It is important to realize that structure is there to guide our lives, but we also have to be adaptable. Learning to adapt is a valuable life skill that helps us to move forward when something has changed.

Reflection: Think about some changes you have seen occur during your lifetime. What are some changes to the structure of society you think will change in the future? What are your reasons for thinking those changes will occur?

DAY 61:

We can obtain peace in our lives when the structures that surround us are steady enough to hold us up and keep us on track while at the same time being flexible enough to change if change is needed without causing our entire world to fall apart. How do we build that kind of structure into our lives? It may sound odd, but we often begin that journey to peace by starting with conflict. It is when we realize things aren't working, that they are in conflict, that we realize we need a change in a current structure. Realizing what is not working, is the first step in trying to figure out what will work.

Reflection: Think about a time you had to change a structure in your life. Was there some conflict that led to the need for the change?

DAY 62:

Often I find when I am in conflict with another person, it isn't that person I'm in conflict but rather the structure that person has put into place that doesn't look like or work for me in a way that my structure does.

I randomly get aggravated at someone for doing something in a way that is different than the way I would do it. I find myself upset with them instead of honoring the fact that they are allowed to set up their structures differently from the way I would set it up.

Letting go of my need to control the structures of other people can be a gift I give to myself and my relationships. It helps to ask in a non-confrontational way, "Just curious, why do you do it in that way?" They probably have a legitimate reason for the structure they have chosen. If not, then you can say, "I wonder if it would work better if….". However, it is important to leave the decision of changing or not changing their structure to them, they have a right to be wrong today.

Reflection: Have you ever watched something someone did in a different way from you and realized their structure might be a better way to do something than your way?

DAY 63:

Sometimes taking a break from our typical structure can be a way to gain new perspective. If life is starting to feel boring or tedious, think about four things you might do differently. Maybe do your work in pencil instead of a pen, mail a letter to a friend instead of sending a text, make a point to talk a little longer than usual to your parents about how school is going, listen to a different radio station for a day. Using a different routine for even a short time helps life to have variety and jolts you into a new sense of awareness.

Reflection: What is something you could do differently today to add variety to your life?

DAY 64:

Releasing negative thoughts or concerns is not only healthy but key to being successful in any other area of your life. Lately, one of the ways I've been working on this is to repeat over and over to myself, "return to positive" when I find myself sinking into a quagmire of negative thinking. It sometimes takes a minute of repetition, but it works to break the power of the negative thoughts that can quickly spiral me down.

Other options include taking a moment to draw or doodle, doing a few minutes of exercise, or turning on some happy music. Anything that can quickly jolt you into a different mental space will remind you that you have control over your thoughts and your life. Moving into higher thoughts will help you to create and maintain a healthy inner structure for your life.

Reflection: What are some ways you could lift your thoughts when you find your thoughts becoming negative?

DAY 65:

20th-century mathematician Benoit Mandelbrot was the first to coin the term, fractal. It originates from the Latin word fractus, which means irregular or fragmented. Fractals are found all around us, especially in nature. A fractal is a simple pattern that repeats itself, becoming more complex the larger it grows. If you have ever looked in a kaleidoscope; you have seen a fractal.

A small fractal can be a metaphor for how structures work. If something is chaotic in a small area like the inside of a locker, it can often be a signal that things are going to get bigger and more complicated on a large scale like your desk, or your bedroom at home. Dealing with the chaos on a small scale can give you the impetus and energy to keep going and organize and clean other areas of your life. So when faced with a problem, remember the lesson of the fractal, start small and build up to solving the bigger issues. All things are connected and when you create positive energy in one area it builds and gives you extra time and brain power to help with more significant issues.

Reflection: What is one small pattern you have seen repeated in other areas of your life?

DAY 66:

Frank Lloyd Wright lived from 1867-1959. He is known as one of the greatest American architects. His unique styles of houses and buildings are still well loved because he made them well-structured and beautiful. One of his buildings was a hotel in Tokyo. In 1923 when Tokyo had its largest earthquake, 140,000 people died, but the Imperial Hotel, which Wright had designed, stood firm and was safe.

When you think of how to structure your life, it is important to anticipate things that might shake up your schedule and leave extra time for them, but it is also important to leave room and space for beauty. The great artist, Pablo Picasso once said, "Art washes away from the soul the dust of everyday life."

You may not have the time to visit an art gallery very often, but art is all around you in many different forms and taking the time to notice it is an excellent way to draw it into your schedule.

Reflection: What are some ways you could include time for art and beauty as a part of the main structure of your life?

DAY 67:

Have you ever tried to do something that required a pattern? Maybe crochet or woodworking? Following a recipe or even the structure of how to write an essay, all require that you pay attention to a master copy so you can repeat the pattern. Learning how to pay close attention is a skill that takes time to learn but will make a difference in your success on any project.

Reflection: What are some ways you can increase your skills of comprehension and paying attention?

DAY 68:

My daughter currently works at a restaurant. When she goes to work, she depends on the people that she is working with to pay attention and follow the structure of what is set up for them in order for things to run smoothly. If someone doesn't do their job, things quickly fall apart for everyone. Learning to follow a structure is a life skill used in every job you will ever have.

Reflection: There are many life skills that you are learning now that will be beneficial later on. What are some ways learning to follow procedures and structures will help you later in your life?

DAY 69:

Having a structure to your life that works well for you is the best way to feel that you have things, "under control" or that you have power over your life. You are always going to have bumps in the road and obstacles that will challenge your structures, but good, basic planning will go a long way to reducing the stress of your life.

Reflection: How have your ideas about the importance of structure changed? Do you feel like you have been able to implement functional structures to help your life flow more smoothly? If not, what things still need to change?

DAY 70:

When people talk about the "break down of society" what they are referring to is the breakdown of stable structures that keep life running smoothly for everyone. Having strong, positive structures where everyone's basic needs are met, is an important part of creating a sustainable world filled with peace. So how do we improve the world around us? Start with choosing peace in your personal life, like the fractals, your peace can spread and make a difference in the lives of people around you.

Reflection: Do you believe reliable structures that promote peace in your life will make a difference in the world? If so, how and why?

POWER UP!

DAY 71:

"Power is of two kinds. One is obtained by the fear of punishment and the other by acts of love. Power based on love is a thousand times more effective and permanent then the one derived from fear of punishment."
-Mahatma Gandhi

Being a good leader is not an easy task. A good leader knows how to lead both by example and by empowering others. A good leader recognizes how to build on the strengths of others while also helping them grow stronger in their areas of weakness. To be a good leader is to challenge yourself to be an effective communicator. Ordering others around and intimidating them may lead to short term success, but long time friendships and effectiveness takes time and a willingness to listen to and work with what team members think is best for the group.

Reflection: Think about people you would consider good leaders. What are some qualities they seem to possess?

DAY 72:

"When the whole world is silent, even one voice becomes powerful." Malala Yousafzai

At 17 years old, Malala Yousafzai was the youngest Nobel Peace Prize winner. Malala knows first-hand that peace can be a challenging and risky choice. Shot in the head when she was 14 years old because of her commitment to speaking to the world about the importance of girls being educated, Malala knew that freedom from fear comes when you decide something you are working for is worth any cost. Her bravery and commitment to education for girls make her a very powerful leader worthy of admiration.

Reflection: Is there an issue that you feel so convicted by that it would be worth leaving your comfort zone to speak boldly about it to the world in whatever way you have available?

DAY 73:

When you can manage the different forces that are impacting your life by giving them structures that make them easier to navigate, you will find that you have a new sense of confidence and power. The power to manage your life successfully is a huge step on the journey to adulthood.

When you realize you always have options, then you can look at what options are best for your life.

For example, you have the option not to do your school work. However, if you choose that option, you also have to be willing to accept the consequences of that choice.

Reflection: Choosing wisely for your life can feel very empowering. What are some choices you have made that have felt like good choices even if you didn't enjoy the work they required?

DAY 74:

"If you realized how powerful your thoughts are, you would never think a negative thought." Peace Pilgrim

When you think of power, the first thing you think of might not be the power of your thoughts, but maybe you should consider this idea. The great philosopher William James once said, "As a man thinketh so is he." Our thoughts shape our attitudes, our attitudes shape our actions, and our actions shape our lives. Think positive isn't just a trite idea, it can be a decision about the type of life you want to live.

Reflection: In what ways do you think taking control of your thoughts might make a difference in your life?

DAY 75:

When you have a task to complete whether it is cleaning your room or finishing a school project, do you feel the need to get someone else's stamp of approval about how good of a job you did or do you look at the completed task and think about how you feel about what you did? Extrinsic rewards like praise, money, stickers and happy faces are nice, but they shouldn't be what motivates you. If it is, then you are giving some of your personal power away to someone else. When you are motivated by your sense of doing the best job you can do; then you recognize that your opinion of yourself is just as important as someone else's opinion about your abilities.

Reflection: Think about a time when you were proud of yourself. In that moment did you need someone else to compliment you or did the feeling of knowing you had done something to the best of your ability increase your sense of personal confidence and power?

DAY 76:

"The most common way people give up their power is by thinking they don't have any." Alice Walker

Alice Walker is the well-known author of *The Color Purple*, a book about racism in America. What is not as well known about Alice Walker is that she became permanently blind in her right eye as a result of being shot with a BB gun. Scar tissue around her eye and the teasing she received caused Alice to become painfully shy and self-conscious. Alice started writing poems and stories to cope with her inner pain. Eventually, she turned her pain into promise as winning the approval of her peers, she also became valedictorian and was voted most popular girl of her senior class.

When Alice was a young teenager, she must have felt like she didn't have any power. What a blessing to the world that she realized her strength and used her talents to write and work as an activist for others.

Reflection: What are some ways that people give up their power and what do you think are some ways they might reclaim their power?

DAY 77:

"Calmness is the cradle of power." Josiah Gilbert Holland

The reason mindfulness activities like meditation, prayer, or taking a long walk are so important is because they allow us time to return to a place of calm when life becomes overwhelming. When your mind is racing, it is hard to feel like you have any personal power or choice in your life at all, but if you can find a way to return to your center, to still your thoughts, and be in a peaceful place, things quickly become more manageable and calm.

When you take time daily to refocus yourself, everything else in your life becomes a little easier to accomplish. Regular time for reflection and stilling your mind is a habit that will create new joy, energy, and power for everything else you attempt.

Reflection: What are ways that you return yourself to a place of calmness and peace when your thoughts become overwhelming?

DAY 78:

"Most powerful is he who has himself in his own power."
Lucius Annaeus Seneca

Seneca was a philosopher and a tutor for the great
Roman emperor, Nero. As Seneca watched Nero's
emotional decline, he understood the importance of being
able to have self-control. Regardless of how much control
Nero had of his country it was his inability to control
himself that led to his demise.

Having a strong sense of inner peace about who you are,
starts with knowing that you are the only one ultimately
responsible for you. Your learning is yours, and your
actions are yours. Take time to think about the decisions
you are making for your life, do they reflect the type of
person you want to be on a daily basis?

Reflection: What are some ways that you have power over
your life?

DAY 79:

"It's really a wonder that I haven't dropped all my ideals, because they seem so absurd and impossible to carry out. Yet I keep them, because in spite of everything I still believe that people are really good at heart." -Anne Frank

When the Nazi's took power in the early 1940's, there was a young girl named Anne Frank that went into hiding with her parents. Anne Frank went from being a fun, lively teenager enjoying school with her friends to a quiet life going into hiding with her family, to eventually dying at a young age in a concentration camp. It must have been hard for her to hold on to any sense of optimism about the world, and yet she still believed that deep down there was good in people. Her diary reveals that even in the darkest of days she still found beauty in life. To look at the very worst in life and humankind and choose to see good, is a sign of an unyielding and powerful mind.

Cultivating the habit of seeing good, and choosing to enjoy whatever life serves up to you is a form of power that will transform you and the world. Realizing that you have the authority to choose emotional states like peace and joy instead of thinking they have to be provided for you by an external circumstance, that power to choose, is a life changer. In fact it is a world changer. When you realize your choice to be happy is entirely up to you, it frees you and allows you to enjoy each moment as it comes, not just when it comes in the way you prefer.

Reflection: How does having control over your emotions give you more power in your life?

DAY 80:

"Question: Why are we Masters of our Fate, the captains of our souls? Because we have the power to control our thoughts, our attitudes. That is why many people live in the withering negative world. That is why many people live in the Positive Faith world." Alfred A. Montapert

Invictus (Latin for "unconquered") is a short poem written by the poet William Ernest Henley in 1875. The poem was written during a very difficult time in his life, one of his legs had already been amputated as a result of complications from tuberculosis and he was hoping to save his second leg from being amputated. The poem that includes the lines, "We are masters of our fate, captains of our souls" has gone on to inspire many people including Nelson Mandela, the first black president of South Africa. Both the poet and the president realized that regardless of what life served up to them they had the power to change their circumstances by changing their thought patterns.

Reflection: What type of an impact do you think your everyday thoughts have on your life? Do you think it is possible to have a good life regardless of your outward circumstances?

DAY 81:

"The rules have changed. True power is held by the person who possesses the largest bookshelf, not gun cabinet or wallet." Anthony J. D'Angelo

What do you think the world would be like if that quote were true? How would daily life change? Alexander the Great was known for the extensive libraries he created. His desire to collect the great wisdom from around the world was admirable. It is a very subversive thought (subversive is a fancy word for disruptive) to realize that the world around us is ours to create or destroy.

We change the world through our thoughts and actions. Change may happen slowly, but it can and does happen. If we don't like the things that are happening around us, we can change them. We have the choice to decide for ourselves what power is. Peaceful resistance has happened in many powerful ways across the world throughout time: Martin Luther King, Jr., Gandhi, Malala, none of them had a lot of money or used violence, but they did have a lot of conviction and a lot of personal power. Their choices helped each of them in their own way to make a positive change in the world.

Reflection: What is real power? What qualities do you think of when you think of someone that has a lot of power?

DAY 82:

"Words are singularly the most powerful force available to humanity. We can choose to use this force constructively with words of encouragement, or destructively using words of despair. Words have energy and power with the ability to help, to heal, to hinder, to hurt, to harm, to humiliate and to humble." Yehuda Berg

Often I receive a note or a text from my dear friend Trish that simply says, "I love you. That's all." Those few words have a lot of power to remind me that no matter what is happening, there is someone that believes in me.

Reflection: Think about your conversations on a regular basis, are you making a conscious choice to use your words to build up other people? If you aren't doing this on a regular basis, what are some ways you could be more deliberate about encouraging other people?

DAY 83:

"Knowledge is power. Information is liberating. Education is the premise of progress, in every society, in every family." Kofi Annan

Kofi Annan is a Ghanaian diplomat who served as the seventh Secretary-General of the United Nations from January 1997 to December 2006. Annan and the United Nations were the co-recipients of the 2001 Nobel Peace Prize "for their work for a better organized and more peaceful world."

Why is knowledge power? How does education bring progress to a society? When you look at a painting you may immediately judge that picture based on how the colors or structures impact you based on your past experiences, but when you really learn about a piece of art, what the artist was thinking about, or the message they were trying to get across it really changes how you view that painting.

For example when I realized Degas paintings of ballerinas were a way of showing the value of women that worked hard to perfect their art and had found a way to support themselves through ballet, I stopped seeing them as just pretty pictures. I realized Degas was making an important social statement.

Reflection: Can you think of a time when more knowledge about a topic helped you feel like you had grown, progressed, or had more power?

DAY 84:

"Too often we underestimate the power of a touch, a smile, a kind word, a listening ear, an honest compliment, or the smallest act of caring, all of which have the potential to turn a life around." Leo Buscaglia

One of my personal goals for the past few years has been to deliberately try to become a better listener. I've realized that listening doesn't just involve hearing. Listening is a gift that includes intently looking at someone, thinking about what they are saying (instead of just how you are planning to respond when they finally stop talking) and honoring them as a person.

To be listened to in that manner feels amazing, and to hear in that way actually makes time spent with another person feel more special. We live in a fast-paced world, taking time to listen is a beautiful way to savor life not just spend it. It is to live time instead of kill time.

Reflection: How does active listening make time with another person more meaningful?

DAY 85:

Every day we have plenty of opportunities to get angry, stressed or offended. But what you're doing when you indulge these negative emotions is giving something outside yourself power over your happiness. You can choose to not let little things upset you. It is rare that we look back in life and think, "I wish I would have been more upset about that and thrown a bigger tantrum." Usually we look back at those moments and think, "Ugh, why did I let that situation get the best of me?"

Using your personal power to choose self-control and restraint is a habit you have the opportunity to practice daily.

Reflection: Indulging in negative emotions is like gorging on ice cream on a bad day. It may feel good at the moment, but the extra emotional weight is not worth the energy it takes. What are healthier ways to react when you are angry, stressed or offended?

DAY 86:

"Don't underestimate the power of your vision to change the world. Whether that world is your office, your community, an industry or a global movement, you need to have a core belief that what you contribute can fundamentally change the paradigm or way of thinking about problems." Leroy Hood

Every person that lives has a unique perspective based on their experiences. Your perspective may be just the one needed to solve a problem. I remember once when we invited a homeless man to stay with us for a few days. It happened just when the weather had suddenly turned cold and being in a new house to us we thought the central heat was broken. Before we even had a chance to call someone to fix it, our visitor asked to take a look at it and figured out what we needed to do to fix the heat. Our new friend had not only saved us from being cold but also saved us some money.

From that experience I learned that you never know the gifts other people have to offer. We thought we were helping someone else when in reality he was able to help us even more. I was very glad that our visitor saw that he still had plenty to offer even if he had lost a lot along the way.

Reflection: It can be easy to get depressed and feel like we don't have a lot to offer the world, but each unique perspective is valuable. What is an experience, skill, or something you are enthusiastic about that could help others?

DAY 87:

"Between stimulus and response, there is a space. In that space is our power to choose our response. In our response lies our growth and our freedom." -Viktor E. Frankl

Viktor E. Frankl was an Austrian neurologist, psychiatrist, and a survivor of the Holocaust during World War II. Before being forced into a concentration camp his wife, Tilly Grosser, sewed the pages of the book he had been writing, *Man's Search for Meaning* into the lining of his coat. Soon after, Tilly was sent to a separate concentration camp and guards took Viktor's coat from him. Using whatever scraps of paper he could find he continued to write and reconstruct his book. Liberated after three years in the concentration camp, Viktor wrote and published the book that would come to be known as one of the ten most influential books ever written. The German title of the book, *Nevertheless, Say Yes to Life*, is a strong indicator of the way Frankl felt about his time in the concentration camp.

Frankl believed that the meaning of life can be found in any moment of life, even in the most desperate and disparaging moments, and the hope and freedom of choice that is found within one's own soul is the key to surviving and overcoming trauma.

Reflection: What do you believe brings meaning and purpose to your life? How does your belief impact the choices you make?

DAY 88:
"Pessimism leads to weakness, optimism to power."
William James

William James, known as "the father of psychology" suffered from depression and many physical ailments. It was through his study of philosophy that he overcame much of his depression. His decision to choose thoughts that lifted his attitudes and actions was a first step to helping him deal with his depression. He knew that pessimism or optimism are a result of the constant thoughts one chooses.

Winston Churchill once said, "For myself, I am an optimist—it don't see much use in being anything else."

Reflection: How does having a positive attitude lead to power? If you are a pessimist, how do you think "trying on" optimism for a while would impact your life?

DAY 89:

"When the power of love overcomes the love of power the world will know peace." Jimi Hendrix

One falls in love or increases the love in their life by being deliberate in relationships. Getting to know other people, working with them on projects, spending time together, all of these things happen when you volunteer. Volunteering reminds us that there is something more to life than working for money. Money is neither good nor bad, it is just a tool to help people get what they need in life, but once our basic needs for food and shelter are met, there are higher needs that we don't need money for in order to reach. Those needs for love, friendship, and a feeling of meaning and purpose. can be met through reaching out and volunteering. Volunteering is a way to contribute to society and make the world a better place.

Reflection: What are some ways you have volunteered in the past or would like to volunteer in the future? What are ways that volunteering could increase the power of love in the world?

DAY 90:

"We must develop and maintain the capacity to forgive. He who is devoid of the power to forgive is devoid of the power to love. There is some good in the worst of us and some evil in the best of us. When we discover this, we are less prone to hate our enemies." Martin Luther King, Jr.

Resentment and not being able to forgive are extremely draining. It takes a lot of energy to stay mad at someone. It drains both emotional and physical power, especially if you have buried that resentment deep down. It weighs you down without you even realizing it.

Taking the time and emotional energy it takes to get in touch with your feelings and forgive is a lot like cleaning out your physical spaces, start small and watch how letting go of little resentments gives you more energy to let go of bigger resentments. The beautiful thing is that you can forgive someone else even if they have never asked for your forgiveness. You forgive others because you are the one that benefits.

Reflection: Is there anyone that you have a hard time forgiving? How do you think forgiving would be a benefit to you?

DAY 91:

"Happiness, true happiness, is an inner quality. It is a state of mind. If your mind is at peace, you are happy. If your mind is at peace, but you have nothing else, you can be happy. If you have everything the world can give - pleasure, possessions, power - but lack peace of mind, you can never be happy." Dada Vaswani

In any moment of the day, you can make a conscious decision for peace. It doesn't matter how fast your heart is racing or how quickly you seem to be spiraling downward. You can choose your thoughts. You can choose what to focus on, and that is how you quietly accept happiness.

Reflection: A sunny day at the beach, the way newly mowed grass smells, the feeling of sitting next to a campfire? What are the thoughts, sensations, or memories that bring peace to your heart? How can you collect these thoughts and return to them when you need to bring your mind into a state of peace?

DAY 92:

"There is a sacredness in tears. They are not the mark of weakness, but of power. They speak more eloquently than ten thousand tongues. They are the messengers of overwhelming grief, of deep contrition, and of unspeakable love." Washington Irving

Honestly, I'm probably more likely to cry when I'm exhausted than when I'm feeling a deep emotion. However, there have been times when I have felt something so deeply that I couldn't help but weep. During those times, it is true that our tears carry more power than our words ever could. As your life reaches milestones and turning points, there will be moments when words are inadequate, and your heart overflows. In those moments, there is something extremely powerful and liberating about accepting the grace of the tears that fall. To be confident enough to cry openly and not be ashamed of your deepest feelings is very powerful.

Reflection: Think about the last time you cried because you were experiencing a strong emotion. How can accepting the "grace of tears" be a sign of strength instead of weakness?

DAY 93:

"The world is very different now. For man holds in his mortal hands the power to abolish all forms of human poverty, and all forms of human life." John F. Kennedy

It really isn't such a crazy idea to believe we could create a world in which everyone has enough food and their basic needs are met. We are connected; we have ways to do it. The main things preventing it have less to do with logistics and more to do with conflict and greed.

So how do things change? When things are going badly, what needs to happen to make them right again? It seems like a huge problem, but remember if each person does what he can with what he has; it starts to make a difference. Sometimes the secret is not to look too long at the big picture where you become overwhelmed, but rather to see what you can do where you are and trust that those small acts of goodness will spread.

Reflection: Looking at your resources rather than your lack, what are some things that can be done to help alleviate hunger or poverty in your community?

DAY 94:

"Your problem is how you are going to spend this one odd and precious life you have been issued. Whether you're going to spend it trying to look good and creating the illusion that you have power over people and circumstances, or whether you are going to taste it, enjoy it and find out the truth about who you are." Anne Lamott

Do you consider your life precious? It is. When you think about the things you love, do you put yourself on that list? Sometimes we worry so much about what other people think about us or the kind of impression we are making, we forget to just live. To just enjoy all the amazing things about life. Sunsets, the smell of freshly mown grass, the way kittens or puppies can make us smile, there are so many fun and amazing things to enjoy in the world. Take time to taste, savor, and enjoy your life.

Reflection: When you think about yourself are you always thinking about your faults and your shortcomings, or do you take the time to acknowledge that as a human you have some areas of growth and some areas of strength? How do you think bringing more of a sense of wonder into your life could be helpful in maintaining a sense of balance about your place in the world?

DAY 95:

"Technology gives us power, but it does not and cannot tell us how to use that power. Thanks to technology, we can instantly communicate across the world, but it still doesn't help us know what to say." Jonathan Sacks

Empathy is a fancy word that means you can really feel and understand what another person is feeling. When you can put yourself in another person's place and see the world from their perspective for even a small bit of time, it changes how you feel about them and how you treat them. Learning empathy is a skill that requires a willingness to let go of preconceived notions and really listen to where someone has been and where they are going.

As the world gets smaller, how do you strike up conversation with someone you barely know or don't have a clue about their life? There are two ways to make this easier: ask genuine questions that show you care about them and respect their thoughts, and give them sincere compliments about something you have noticed about them. You develop relationships by coming from a place of empathy, by caring for another person.

Reflection: The world is a mirror reflecting back to us everything we give out, knowing the type of communication you want to receive and be a part of is your first clue about how to treat others. What are some ways you would like someone to treat you if they didn't know you very well?

DAY 96:

"We have become not a melting pot but a beautiful mosaic. Different people, different beliefs, different yearnings, different hopes, different dreams." Jimmy Carter

James Earl "Jimmy" Carter, Jr, was the 39th President of the United States from 1977 to 1981. He was awarded the 2002 Nobel Peace Prize for his work with the Carter Center. When Jimmy Carter left the Oval office and returned to his hometown of Plains, Georgia, he didn't leave behind serving others. He continued to reach out to his community in many ways including building houses with Habitat for Humanity.

His example of service to others is a case of real power. He also knows that to serve others means to respect others, to learn from and trust that we will be stronger if sometimes we agree to disagree. If we appreciate differences instead of trying to abolish differences. Those differences are the beautiful mosaic that makes life colorful and interesting.

Reflection: How does serving others start with respecting them?

DAY 97:

"If we cannot end now our differences, at least we can help make the world safe for diversity." John F. Kennedy

I recently had to find an inexpensive, fast way to cover the main wall of a building. I decided I would try a small art project. I gathered lots of different brightly colored pieces of tissue paper and crumbled them up, and then I smoothed each one back out, so it was textured but a continuous sheet again. Then I glued the pieces of tissue paper onto the wall in lots of different patterns and sizes. The result was a beautiful, colorful wall that brightened up the room and made everyone not only smile but also take pictures in front of it. I titled my art piece, "Unity through Diversity".

When we are willing to embrace diversity instead of sequestering ourselves into groups of people that are just like us, it enriches our lives and helps us to have a greater understanding of the world. We become stronger as individuals and stronger as communities when we appreciate our many different talents, backgrounds, and viewpoints. We don't have to agree with everyone, but showing respect is always a choice and a way to build a safer, saner world. My mom used to tell me that you catch more flies with honey than vinegar. This idiom means that kindness and a good attitude gets us further in life than being sour.

Reflection: What are some ways that diversity can create unity and a safer world?

DAY 98:

"If one does not know to which port he is sailing, no wind is favorable." –Seneca

Have you ever heard of a "vision board"? It is a place where you collect pictures of the types of things you want to experience or achieve in your life. For instance, a photo of a beach might represent an actual place you wish to visit, but also represent what you would like to feel when you are there: peace, relaxation, a calm spirit. Creating a vision board is a way to direct your thoughts. Directing your thoughts is a way to start directing your actions like figuring out a way to get to the beach or a place to stay when you get there. Our visions create our thoughts, our thoughts create our actions, and our actions create our lives.

Reflection: If you were to create a vision board for your life what are some pictures you would like to have on it?

DAY 99:

"It's all about the pie." –p.e.p.s.

When I was in college, I was dealing with some tough emotional issues from my childhood. As a result, I started seeing a counselor to help me work through a lot of the pain and confusion that I was having a difficult time understanding on my own. During the sessions, I didn't feel like our conversations were helping me all that much. However after each session, I would go to a local pie shop and choose a piece of pie that looked fantastic. I would sit down by myself and enjoy it while I thought about everything I had learned from the session.

It was a time in my life when I had become an incredible people pleaser to win the approval of everyone around me. Taking time to buy and eat a delicious piece of pie was a way for me to say, "I'm also worth an investment!" Through the counseling and pie sessions, I slowly learned that my opinions, thoughts, actions, all mattered. I was learning to honor my power instead of giving it all away. I was learning to make decisions based on what was good for me as well as good for others.

Reflection: Do you honor your opinions about things? When you strive to make others happy are you also balancing your life so you are not feeling unhappy?

DAY 100:

"Your life experiences are great teachers, but if you don't realize that you're in class, you may miss the entire course. Sure, it will be offered again, but you know what happens to tuition every year!" Bruce I. Doyle III, Ph.D.

One of the amazing joys of life is that it is a constant learning experience. We get to learn all sorts of practical things like how to do algebra, (which believe it or not you actually will use in all kinds of unexpected ways). How to create an effective presentation, how to write essays, as well as deep emotional lessons like how to get along with people that irritate us, how to love ourselves, how to know when to let go and when to hang on. All those lessons come to us in many different shapes, sizes, and disguises.

Part of leading a life that builds up your inner power and strength has to do with appreciating and recognizing the lessons offered to us. Everything, everything, everything can be learned from, even the things that are awkward and uncomfortable can teach us if we are willing to learn instead of playing hooky, or mentally blocking them out. Life has a way of being a persistent teacher. If we don't pay attention, the same lessons show up over and over usually with harder consequences if we don't learn from them.

Reflection: Take time to think about experiences that seem to happen to you a lot. Good or bad, what do you think you could learn from those experiences to keep or change the outcome?

DAY 101: Eulogy for my dad:

"There are several things I will always remember about Daddy. The biggest was that he loved to serve and service was his love language. My mother almost always got breakfast in bed. On Saturday mornings when I was a child, my dad would always wake up early and drive downtown to buy me fresh donuts and cinnamon rolls to enjoy with Saturday morning cartoons.

My dad was often falling as you know, it sort of became a family joke, but I think the hardest he ever fell was in love with my mother. Two years ago I spent some time with my parents and after we said goodbye we dropped someone off and then drove back by my parents' house. There was my dad in his wheelchair watching my mom playing with her flowers in the front yard. There was a total look of love and admiration on his face, and the CD in the car was playing John Lennon's song, "Come Grow Old With Me, the Best is Yet to Be..." It was a perfect snow globe moment of how I will always remember my parents.

My father was a wise man, and the advice he gave very sparingly to me I always remembered, like don't forget to change the oil in your car, and your husband most of all needs to know that you respect him, and get a good education, it will be worth it to you. He had many faults but always tried his best, and perhaps this was the best lesson he could have shared with me."

This was part of the eulogy I wrote when my dad died. A eulogy is a way to honor and remember someone's life. Thinking about the way someone might deliver your eulogy is an interesting way to begin with the end in mind.

Reflection: When your life comes to a close (hopefully at the ripe old age of 120 or so) what do you want people to remember about you? What things do you want to accomplish that people will discuss? What character traits do you wish to possess that people will think about when they think of you?

DAY 102:

"As we look ahead into the next century, leaders will be those who empower others." Bill Gates

To empower another person means to help them see their value and worth, to help them understand that they have the power within themselves to be successful. Maria Montessori believed that a teacher should never do for a child what they could do for themselves. Having the knowledge and ability to take care of yourself is very empowering.

Reflection: What are some ways you can help empower the people around you?

DAY 103:

A standard light bulb and a compact fluorescent light bulb both give light. One just gives their light with less of an energy drain on the electrical system. When you look at your life are you using your power and light as efficiently as you can? If you feel emotionally and physically drained at the end of the day, it might be a sign that the answer is no. Think about what you can do to be more efficient at the different tasks in your life.

Reflection: Being a light to those around you starts with taking good care of yourself, so you have enough power to be effective. What are some healthy habits that will help you shine brightly?

DAY 104:

When I refer to my dog as a "watch dog" I don't mean that he is protective of me or the house, in fact, he will wag his tail when anyone comes near the house. I mean that he literally seems to have an uncanny ability to tell time. I could probably set my watch to his bark that starts at 6:30 a.m. every morning and 4:45 every night. He barks one sharp bark every few minutes until I come out and give him his food.

My dog knows the power of persistence. He knows that if he continues his one bark on a consistent basis, then I will eventually come out to feed him. I know that the sooner I feed him, the sooner he will be quiet.

Reflection: Is there something in your life right now that applying the power of persistence might help you complete the task?

DAY 105:

Sometimes you need to power up in your life, and sometimes you need to power down. When you have a lot to accomplish it may be helpful to give it an extra push to help you finish, but other times you are so tired that you need to take a break and start fresh on the project to really do a good job. Learning when to power up and when to power down can make all the difference.

Reflection: When are some times in your life that it makes more sense to power up and when does it make sense to power down?

DAY 106:

What does it mean to you to "make a difference in the world"? Does it have to be something big? You may find that small things can make a bigger difference than you realize. Here is a list of some minor changes you might make in your life that could lead to big differences:

1. Recycle
2. Once a week write a note to someone to tell them how much you appreciate them.
3. Notice how many people walk through the door in the morning smiling. Is there a way you could cheer up those that aren't smiling?
4. Keep up with your pencil or pen every day. Taking care of something small empowers you to take better care of everything in your life.
5. Make an effort to learn about good things happening in the world and share those ideas with others. Lifting everyone's thoughts and moods can make a huge difference.

Reflection: What are some small things you could do that would have a bigger impact in the world?

DAY 107:

"There is nothing in a caterpillar that tells you it's going to be a butterfly." Buckminster Fuller

The potential that exists in every single one of us is extraordinary. The best way to help it come into being is by affirming the good we see in each other. Each day there will be opportunities for you to tell the people around you something wonderful you have noticed about them. Do it. Be amazed by how all the good you notice leads to even more good.

Reflection: What are some wonderful traits you have noticed about someone near you? What is stopping you from telling them what you have noticed? What difference do you think it might make if you did tell them?

DAY 108:

"Never forget that you are one of a kind. Never forget that if there weren't any need for you in all your uniqueness to be on this earth, you wouldn't be here in the first place. And never forget, no matter how overwhelming life's challenges and problems seem to be, that one person can make a difference in the world. In fact, it is always because of one person that all the changes that matter in the world come about. So be that one person."   R. Buckminster Fuller

When we doubt our importance in the world, it can be helpful to remember all the different combinations of traits that make our individual life important. It can also be helpful to remember people that faced great obstacles but later found success:

1.   Bill Gates first company failed.
2.   Albert Einstein didn't speak until he was four years old.
3.   The comedian and actor Jim Carey had to drop out of school when he was fifteen to help support his family when his dad became unemployed. For a while, they were homeless and lived in a van.
4.   Vincent Van Gogh only sold one painting during his lifetime.

Reflection: What are some traits that you have that make you unique from the people around you? How can those traits help you face obstacles?

DAY 109:

Albert Einstein once stated that he didn't have any special talent, he was just passionately curious. Curiosity about the world around you is an important quality to develop. Thinking about how things work or don't work can lead you to a life's purpose and passion.

Reflection: What are some things that make you curious? How could you learn more about them?

DAY 110:

Albert Lexie built a shoe shine box in his eighth-grade shop class. That small box was the basis for his career as a shoe shiner for thirty years at the Children's Hospital of Pittsburg. Being someone that shines shoes sounds like a very humble career, and indeed, Albert Lexie led an ordinary life. It was that humble life that allowed him the chance to give away about $200,000 worth of tips he made as a shoe shiner. He donated his tips to the Free Care Fund for patients at the Children's Hospital. His story has been an inspiration to many; he has been inducted into the Hall of Fame for Caring Americans by the Caring Institute in 2006, honored by People magazine, and even had a book written about him.

Being a person that makes a powerful difference doesn't require a lot, what it does require is caring and doing what you can with what you have, no matter how small it may seem.

Reflection: Do you think Albert realized what a difference he would make when he first started donating his tips? Would you consider him an everyday hero?

DAY 111:

How old do you have to be to make a dynamic change in the world? Ask Joshua Williams. Joshua was five years old when he created the non-profit organization, "Joshua's Heart". This organization works to create an awareness of, and help people that go hungry every day in America. One in every seven households in America suffers from food instability. Not having enough healthy food is a problem especially for preschool and school aged children. According to Joshua's website, today in America statistics show that a majority of school-aged students (51 %) live in homes where healthy food may not be available. Worldwide poor nutrition is responsible for 45 % of deaths for children under the age of five.

Joshua Williams is now a young teen, and his organization has helped distribute more than 500,000 pounds of healthy food to people in need and, even more important, it has helped raised awareness of hunger in America.

Reflection: Think about how crazy it must have seemed for five-year-old Joshua to want to do something to change hunger in America, then reflect on the difference it has made for him to follow his crazy dream.

DAY 112:

"Begin doing what you want to do now. We are not living in eternity. We have only this moment, sparkling like a star in our hand-and melting like a snowflake…"   -Sir Frances Bacon

The idea of power encompasses many things: the power to change, the power to make a difference, the power to give, the power to choose, powering up, powering down, using your power, losing your power, using the most of your power, empowering others, empowering yourself, and the list continues. How much power you have is not as important as how you use the power you have. You have this brilliant moment to start using your power in a way you are proud of when this moment turns into last year or twenty years ago.

Reflection: What are some ways you have discovered that you use your personal power? What are some ways you would like to use it in the future?

CHANGE IS THE ONLY CONSTANT

DAY 113:

Some people love change and some people fear change, but inevitably change happens. When the hero receives a new call in their life, it means things are about to change. Being able to deal with change in healthy ways will go a long way in helping the hero to feel good about the journey. Some changes may feel negative, like a friend moving away or being put in a group of people that you don't know well or feel that you don't share a lot in common. Some changes may feel great like getting a teacher that you always wanted to have, or being chosen to be on the student council or a sports team. Whether the change is perceived as positive or negative may even change as you find out more information. When change happens it is best to approach it with a gentle attitude, maybe the way you would approach a dog or cat that you have never met. Time may prove that the change is better than you expected. Keeping your heart open is a good way to make sure change happens as smoothly as possible.

Reflection: Is there a change you have experienced in your life that you feel you handled well? If so, what was helpful to you?

DAY 114:

One of the reasons change can be scary is because we often feel out of control. When change happens, there are several coping techniques you can use to make the journey easier. One of them is to take the time to absorb the new change. Giving yourself time to understand more about the situation will help you see what things you have control over and what things you don't. The main thing you always have control over is your attitude. If you choose to focus on the positive aspects of the situation, even if there seems to be more negative than positive, you may be surprised how the change appears to be less intimidating.

Reflection: Having control of our thoughts about any experience will help us develop the courage we need to face change. What is a positive about a change you are currently facing?

DAY 115:

When change happens, it can sometimes be a lot to absorb in the beginning. It can even be a source of anxious feelings. Knowing different ways to cope with stress whether it is positive or negative pressure will give you options to help keep you from getting stuck on your path. Maybe you are very kinesthetic and need to exercise to clear your head; sometimes it is helpful just to get outside and enjoy some sunshine to help get a different perspective. For some people writing their feelings or drawing can help them cope with change, other people need someone they can talk to and discuss alternatives. Knowing yourself can help you be more resilient when changes come your way.

Reflection: What are some ways that you cope with stress? Are there any new things you could add to your tool bag to help you that you may not have tried before?

DAY 116:

Proactive change is when you realize something is not working for you, and you want to do something different. Maybe you realize you need to be more organized, or would like to be more outgoing. Perhaps you wish to learn more about how to handle money or learn a new skill.

When seeking out advice about how to do something differently, it isn't a sign of weakness, it means you are smart enough to realize your limitations and know the answer is available if the right questions are asked. Life is frequently about finding the right question to ask rather than the right answer. Finding the right question means clarifying in your mind what information you want to know. In that process, you often discover your answer before you even have to ask the question.

Reflection: What questions feel immense and significant in your life right now?

DAY 117:

"The secret of change is to focus all of your energy, not on fighting the old, but on building the new." –Quote from the character "Socrates" in Dan Millman's book The Way of the Peaceful Warrior.

When we reach a decision that our life is not working for one reason or another, how do we keep limiting thought patterns and bad habits from holding us back? We choose what we want to change and focus our thoughts on how we can make that a reality in our lives.

All of us have a tremendous amount of chatter going on in our heads all day long. Taking control of that chatter and focusing our thoughts on what we want to change allows us to let go of any limiting thoughts that would hold us back. I usually follow a simple formula for changing my thoughts and my life. If a thought is weighing me down, I objectively examine it and consider whether or not it is beneficial. Often it isn't, it is just a thought that has become wedged into my head, and it needs to be eradicated. The way I do this is to focus on what about that situation feels positive to me and concentrate on the positive. Everything has a positive side, sometimes you have to dig deeper to think of it, but it is there.

Reflection: All thoughts carry a certain amount of emotional weight to them. You are the one that gets to decide if you want to go on thinking heavy, depressing thoughts or if you want to choose lighter thoughts. Time will pass either way, which one do you think would lead to a happier, more productive life?

DAY 118:

"Everyone thinks of changing the world, but no one thinks of changing himself."   Leo Tolstoy

If we take note, we often find that the world seems to act like a mirror reflecting back to us the very actions we are doing ourselves. If everyone you encounter seems impatient, it may be that you are impatient without realizing it. Slowing down to think about the things that happen around you is a good way to see how your actions might be causing chain reactions without you being aware of them. If the things you are seeing are negative, you can make the choice to do the opposite in your life. Consider it an experiment, change your actions to see if the people around you start becoming more patient, or more helpful.

Reflection: Think about the encounters you have with other people on a regular basis, are they mostly positive? Are there any ways that you have noticed the world mirroring back the actions you send into the world? When you are in a good mood, do most other people seem to be smiling back at you? When you are grouchy, does it seem other people are grouchy too?

DAY 119:

"Never believe that a few caring people can't change the world. For, indeed, that's all who ever have." Margaret Mead

Have you ever thought about the different ways that people have made the world a better place? When a culture sees a dramatic change, what is it that causes it to happen? Often it starts with one person or a small group that believe passionately in a concept, and their passion spreads.

Reflection: Think about some major culture changes that have occurred in the world. What were the reasons for those changes? What are some changes you would like to see happen in the future?

DAY 120:

Ever since you were a small child, people have probably asked you, "What do you want to do when you grow up?"

Usually, when people ask that question they want to know what type of career you would like to have someday, but I'd like to challenge you to think of that question differently. It seems more important to ask, "What do you want to change, learn, and experience when you grow up?" This question helps you to consider a wider variety of options for your life.

It helps you to look around and see what things you are passionate about and the many ways you could be of service to the world through those interests. It helps you consider all the things you would need to learn to make a difference or live the type of life you are most interested in living. It's helpful to see a variety of careers that might fit into the category you are thinking of and even consider how knowledge in one career could be built on to lead to another career. The more you can open up your options the more you will be able to navigate efficiently through systems to reach your goals.

Reflection: What if you had a magic mirror that reflected back to you not the person you are now, but the person you will be? What would you like to see? What items would be in the background of the mirror image?

DAY 121:

"Very often a change of self is needed more than a change of scene." -A. C. Benson

It is easy to daydream that if only you were in a different place or had different circumstances, or didn't have to deal with a particular person, that life would be easier and more enjoyable. Sometimes that is true, but more often than not the joy of a change of scenery doesn't last long because no matter where you go, there you are. In other words, often the problems we are facing have more to do with our approach to the issues than the concerns themselves.

The hard work of looking within to see what attitudes or actions we do have the ability to change in order to transform our lives is a task most people would rather avoid. It's a lot easier to complain than to change. However, just accepting that it is difficult but possible is a great first step. Take baby steps. Make goals. Write them down. Look at them often. Realize that you have the potential to be your own best friend, and that best friends tell you what you need to hear, not just what you want to hear.

Reflection: Start thinking about your complaints, are there any that a change of self would be just as effective if not more effective than a change of scenery?

DAY 122:

"The curious paradox is that when I accept myself just as I am, then I can change." -Carl Rogers

Carl Rogers was a psychologist and peace activist. His theories of personal development, being an effective teacher, and reducing conflict have been studied all over the world.

He knew that self-acceptance is crucial to being able to move forward in a healthy manner in life, but he also applied the concept to relationships. His approach to resolving conflict involved having each person involved restate the other person's position until they both agreed that they were on the same page. It is this striving to first understand rather than be understood that leads to harmony. On a personal level, you have to accept yourself in order to change, on a relationship level, it is knowing that someone else understands and values your inherent worth that lets you let go of your defenses and move forward to acceptable compromises.

Reflection: What are some areas where you have a difficult time accepting yourself just as you are? What are some ways to embrace self-acceptance?

DAY 123:

"All changes, even the most longed for, have their melancholy; for what we leave behind us is a part of ourselves; we must die to one life before we can enter another." -Anatole France

Growing up is the process of leaving behind parts of yourself in order to discover other parts of yourself. It can be exciting, but also a little sad. Sometimes these changes happen so gradually you don't even realize them. At one time the favorite toy that you played with every day becomes an item on your shelf you rarely notice anymore. Or a ritual that happened on a daily basis like your mom reading bedtime stories just slowly fades away.

Accepting that change happens means accepting that life is unfolding as it should, that natural rites of passage just happen. That acceptance is what allows us to move forward and become the new person we are meant to become.

Reflection: Are there any changes in your immediate future that will require you to leave parts of yourself behind? Are there any plans you could make to make those changes easier to accept?

DAY 124:

"When you blame others, you give up your power to change." -Robert Anthony

Being able to say, "You're right, that was my mistake or poor choice." Is remarkably freeing when it is the truth. If it is genuinely your problem, admitting your fault allows you to figure out a solution or make amends with others quickly and move on to make a better choice the next time. Looking around for someone else to blame not only wastes time but makes you look untrustworthy.

Reflection: How does quickly accepting responsibility when you have done something wrong make the situation easier?

DAY 125:

"Life is about not knowing, having to change, taking the moment and making the best of it, without knowing what's going to happen next." -Gilda Radner

Gilda Radner was a beloved comedian and actress best known for the hilarious characters she created on the TV show Saturday Night Live. She knew a thing or two about improvisational theater, which is making up a scene with a group of actors based on the situation as you go rather than following a script.

Most of life is improv. Being able to go with the flow of what is happening rather than lamenting that there is no script to follow is key to being able to enjoy life and make the most of your time.

Reflection: How does making the best of the moment, changing gears quickly if you need to, allow you to enjoy life more?

DAY 126:

"Could we change our attitude, we should not only see life differently, but life itself would come to be different."
-Katherine Mansfield

I once had a student that was constantly complaining about how unfair his life was and how much school work I was giving him. One day I turned to him and quietly said, "You are absolutely right, life isn't fair. There are thousands of kids living in complete poverty in war-torn areas of the world that would give anything to be sitting in your seat with an opportunity to learn and get a good education."

Those statements changed his perspective and his attitude. He went from being a disruptive student to being an A student, and last I heard he is on track to attend medical school.

Reflection: Are there any negative attitudes that you currently indulge in that might change by changing your perspective?

DAY 127:

"When it becomes more difficult to suffer than to change... you will change." -Robert Anthony

There can be many reasons why someone finally decides to make a change in their life but often change doesn't occur until what we are doing causes us so much pain or annoyance that we are unwilling to continue in the same manner.

It can also be hard to watch someone else that you know would be happier if they would change in some way but they don't seem to be able to grasp the need or reached the point where they think change is necessary.

Accepting that just like you, everyone has their levels of tolerance or intolerance for anything can be very freeing. Letting go of your need to help someone else make their situation better can be a gift to them. It tells them that you trust their ability and power to change their life on their terms.

Reflection: Instead of always trying to help them, are there times in your life or the lives of others that backing away might be a bigger help to them?

DAY 128:

"It takes as much energy to wish as it does to plan."
— Eleanor Roosevelt

T.E.A. is an acronym for Thoughts, Emotions, Actions. When our thoughts and imagination have given us a direction to go in, and our emotions are in a congruent, excited state about what we are planning, then it is time to take action. A wish can be a good starting point, but then it needs to be broken down into manageable strategies of how to make that dream come true.

Reflection: What are some steps you could take to change one of your desires into a reality?

DAY 129:

"Serve the dinner backward, do anything - but for goodness sake, do something weird." -Elsa Maxwell

I'm not sure it's necessary to serve dinner backward, although life is uncertain and eating dessert first may be a good idea. A better idea is to make sure you make the effort in life to keep things interesting. Plan days where you visit a new place or learn something new. Your brain needs to be challenged, and life is more enjoyable when you have new opportunities.

Reflection: What is something you could do differently to make life more stimulating today?

DAY 130:

You know that feeling that comes right before a school break? When you are so ready to be "away from everyone"? When it seems like no matter what, everyone is just slightly getting on your nerves? When all you want is a change of scene and routine?

If your break can't seem to come quick enough, it may be a sign that you need mental and physical rest. Sometimes that just means going to bed an hour earlier or taking the time to journal or listen to your thoughts. The change you are seeking may be your need to withdraw from the world so you can reconnect with your soul.

Reflection: What are ways you can relax and unwind even when you can't physically change where you are?

DAY 131:

"Every great dream begins with a dreamer. Always remember, you have within you the strength, the patience, and the passion to reach for the stars to change the world."
-Harriet Tubman

Harriet Tubman depended on the stars to help her guide runaway slaves to freedom. During her life, she faced danger over and over again to do what she felt was the right thing. Tubman knew that living wouldn't be living if she wasn't doing what she could to help others. She had to follow her calling regardless of the personal risks.

Reflection: Are there any dreams that stir your soul? Stars that seem out of reach but are there to guide your path?

DAY 132:

When we are judgmental of other people, it is often because there is something about them that we don't like in ourselves. Some aspect of what we don't like in them is also an aspect of something we fear or dislike about ourselves. It may not manifest in the same way, but if you look deep, you will find that the root is the same. For instance, you might despise someone because they are stingy with their money only to find when you reflect, that you have a way that you are equally stingy: maybe with your time, with your possessions, or with your emotional energy.

If world peace were to ever occur in the world, I believe it would start with a worldwide wave of self-compassion. A realization that our flaws have many reasons and many reactions. Those flaws that drive us crazy may be the very things that are meant to be there to take us to a higher place. It was because I struggled with my temper that I started studying about peace. I wanted to know how to be calm under pressure instead of reacting in negative ways under pressure. Do I still struggle with this? Occasionally, but less and less. Having self-compassion offers me a way to deal with my emotions instead of expending so much energy just trying to control them.

Reflection: What are ways that having more self-compassion might change your life?

DAY 133:

At some point in my life I started making it a habit to have my first thought of the morning be some variation of this idea, "Today is going to be a great day, good things are going to happen and I'm thankful for this day."

It is an encouraging way to start the day, an optimistic hope for what the day may hold. Even on the worse days when you look back at the entire day, you have at least a few things to be truly thankful for in your life.

Make it a habit to look for beautiful things to happen. It might be the way the sun rises over the clouds, a small flower between the cracks of the sidewalk, or a hug from a friend. Every day there is something to be grateful for if you are willing to look.

Reflection: What do you think the impact would be in your life if you look for something to be thankful for every day?

DAY 134:

Sometimes you seem to get stuck dealing with the same type of annoying person or situation over and over in your life. Once you recognize the pattern, it helps to take a deep, deep breath and realize there is something to be learned from what you are avoiding. The quicker you learn it, the quicker you can move past it.

Reflection: Are there any annoying situations or people with the same personality type that you seem to run into over and over? Why do you try to avoid them? What are some reasons or ways you could appreciate rather than run from them?

DAY 135:

"Forgiving does not erase the bitter past. A healed memory is not a deleted memory. Instead, forgiving what we cannot forget creates a new way to remember. We change the memory of our past into a hope for our future." -Lewis B. Smedes

Forgiving a situation is a gift of peace that we give to ourselves. It allows us to see a situation in a new light, a light that is softer and less painful to remember. It reframes the picture we have been looking at and allows us to see it from a different perspective.

Reflection: Do you have any memories that are painful for you to remember? Is there anyone, including yourself, that you need to forgive so the memory can be less traumatic for you?

DAY 136:

A proactive way to create positive change in your life is to think about the type of life you would like to be living ten years from now, and then five years from now. What things need to happen to create the lifestyle you want to live? Some things happen by chance, but most things need to have some deliberate planning to help you get where you want to go smoothly.

Reflection: What are some tangible things you would like to be doing or accomplished ten years from now? Pretend that those ten years have already passed. Write a letter to your current self. What things can you imagine happening that your future self would tell you about that made your desires for the future come true?

DAY 137:

No matter what age you are, your body is going through changes. Getting use to your body reacting in different ways or having to buy different clothes because you have grown or transformed in some way is sometimes fun, but also sometimes annoying. Accepting change with grace is also a way of saying that you accept yourself and honor the time period of life you are currently experiencing.

Reflection: How can accepting that physical changes are normal and expected help you to not stress about them as much?

DAY 138:

When you make a poor choice for your life or behavior, it may be because of brain chemistry and being stuck in the amygdala part of the brain, so you are in a fight or flight mode. Circumventing these poor choices may be easier than you think. It starts with realizing you are anxious so you can calm down and remind yourself that you are safe, that you can handle whatever is in front of you. Taking the extra few minutes to breathe deeply so your brain and emotions can catch up and realize you are safe is a habit that might be life changing.

Reflection: Practicing breathing deeply and affirming that you are safe is a habit you can do when you are even slightly stressed to help it become the first response when you are in more intense situations. When are some times that you feel stressed that will allow you to practice this skill?

DAY 139:

Sometimes in life, you just feel stuck, unable to move forwards or even care enough to try. Be gentle with yourself. A moment in time doesn't define a life. Find someone you can talk with, find a way to get the feelings that are stuck on the inside out of your mind. Move around some of your belongings. Read a funny book. Get a coloring page and color. Go outside and take a walk or ride your bike. But most of all, be gentle with yourself. Think kind thoughts.

Reflection: Don't get too worried if you start to feel "stuck" in life, just take it as a chance to slow down and reflect, see if any new opportunities or paths are waiting for you that you have been too busy to notice.

DAY 140:

As a teen you may find that your shoes are suddenly too small, your arms seem too long, and you feel off balance by your quickly changing body. The physical changes are equally matched by the changes in your temperament, one moment you are cool as a cucumber and the next you're blowing your top, and you have no idea what set you off to make you so upset.

Dealing with hormones that have you feeling way up or way down can be very difficult, but also very normal. It helps to realize that almost everyone that has gone through the teen years has gone through the same up and down mood swings. Having a sense of perspective can help you relax about it when things seem overwhelming. It helps to have a mentor to talk with. Your mentor can be very helpful to just figure out the changes you are facing.

Reflection: What changes are you going through right now that are difficult, but also perfectly normal?

DAY 141:

Helen Keller lived from 1880 to 1968, in spite of being both deaf and blind she went on to earn a bachelor's degree and became a leading advocate for women's suffrage, rights for people with disabilities, and many other social issues. She never felt that her way of experiencing the world was an excuse to not try and make things better for herself and others.

Reflection: Do you think Helen Keller's life would have been different if she hadn't had challenges to overcome?

DAY 142:

J.K. Rowling is the well-known author of the Harry Potter books. One magical object that is mentioned in the Harry Potter books is The Mirror of Erised, which doesn't show a person's reflection, but rather the deepest desire of their heart (as you may have guessed, Erised is desire spelled backward).

J.K. Rowling may have had many desires before her novels were published. She was a single mother on welfare, and her books were rejected several times before they were published. Can you imagine being one of the publishing houses that turned her down after they saw her tremendous success?

Daydreaming can be a wonderful thing, providing a way for us to imagine a future we haven't seen yet, but it is important not to get so stuck in thinking about our desires that we don't make any progress towards making them a reality.

Reflection: What are some steps that you imagine J.K. Rowling had to take to help her desires become reality?

DAY 143:

Elizabeth Fry (1780-1845) was a Quaker woman that became aware of the unsanitary and deplorable conditions in English prisons in her early thirties. She began working to make changes in the prison system by starting with bringing in clean clothes and teaching hygiene to encourage prisoners to improve their lives. Her programs and work as an advocate brought about many prison reforms. She believed that working to end poverty and social injustice were critical to creating a better world.

Her contribution to the world centered on being willing to tackle subjects that were uncomfortable for other people. Her commitment to this task led to the beginning of prison reforms. She also established a homeless shelter and created a nursing school. Several of the nurses that studied there went on to work with Florence Nightingale.

Reflection: Elizabeth Fry saw a need for change and did what she could to make a difference. What are some tactics she might have used to make people willing to discuss topics they would have rather ignored?

DAY 144:

"Gratitude unlocks the fullness of life. It turns what we have into enough, and more. It turns denial into acceptance, chaos to order, confusion to clarity. It can turn a meal into a feast, a house into a home, a stranger into a friend. Gratitude makes sense of our past, brings peace for today and creates a vision for tomorrow." -Melody Beattie

It is amazing how a change in perspective can change your whole world, and gratitude is the easiest way to change your perspective.

Reflection: Every moment of your life you can look around and find reasons to be grateful. What do you think happens that causes us to forget this? What are some ways to develop an attitude of gratitude?

DAY 145:

Brothers Bert and John Jacobs grew up in a noisy household of six kids. When they were very young, their parents were in a serious car wreck. Their mother had a few broken bones, and their dad lost his right hand. Their father developed a harsh temper, yelled a lot, and things were often difficult in their home. To counteract all of this, their mother made it a habit of asking each of her six kids to tell her something good that had happened during their day. Her optimism during trying times had a profound impact on the two brothers who later went on to found the Life Is Good company with a brand of t-shirts and other products.

The company which sells products featuring a character named Jake that has a happy attitude about all life has to offer, got its start after a conversation the brothers had about how the mainstream media makes its money by feeding on people's fears. The Jacob brothers were convinced that people needed a hero whose only super power was his positive attitude about life. Jake was born, and the brothers quickly went from living in their van to creating a $100 million dollar company.

Reflection: Bert and John realized the power of optimism to change their world and used that power to remind others that life is good. What are some ways that you think life is good today?

DAY 146:

"Everybody can be great. Because anybody can serve. You don't have to have a college degree to serve. You don't have to make your subject and your verb agree to serve.... You don't have to know the second theory of thermodynamics in physics to serve. You only need a heart full of grace. A soul generated by love."
-Martin Luther King, Jr. Minister, Civil Rights Activist

Education is vital, but it can only take you so far. The biggest part of being an everyday hero is about having the right attitude. An attitude that helps you look around at the world see what needs to be done, and using what you have to make a difference.

Reflection: What qualities and attitudes do you think are necessary to live the life of an everyday hero?

EQUILIBRIUM

DAY 147:

"Balance in all things doesn't mean balance in your actions, but balance within. When you are balanced and at one with yourself, your actions will reflect your inner serenity. Stop giving yourself expectations and an ideal to live up to. Stop thinking of the outcome. Surrender to your instincts, your heart, and your faith. Doing what feels harmonious with your true feelings is always the right decision."
— Lacey M.

Taking time to be still and listen to the guidance of your own heart is as restful and productive as taking the time to sleep. Slowing down to just receive instead of constantly being busy sounds counterproductive, but it allows your brain the opportunity to focus and bring to the surface the ideas and actions that will be the most helpful in accomplishing your goals and changing your life.

Reflection: While it seems like letting go and daydreaming would be easy, sometimes you have to make time for it or your schedule gets too busy and your time gets eaten up by unimportant activities. When are some points in your day when you could take a break to be still and calm?

DAY 148:

"Don't confuse symmetry with balance."
— Tom Robbins, Even Cowgirls Get the Blues

My husband is a sculptor, and one of his favorite things to do as an artist is to create large-scale sculptures that don't look like they would balance, but do balance. When I see his sculptures, I'm in awe of how he can stabilize things that seem like they would fall over if given the slightest touch.

When looking at life, I discover that balance is not necessarily created because things are exactly the same. Balance occurs when emotional weight is distributed in such a way that everything works out evenly, and you are feeling positive about the way you are spending your time, energy, and meeting your obligations. It takes frequent readjusting to your schedule to clarify how you best want to spend your most precious resources: your time and your energy.

Reflection: Does your life feel in balance right now? What are some things that need to be adjusted in your life to help them feel more balanced?

DAY 149:

"There are moments when I wish I could roll back the clock and take all the sadness away, but I have a feeling that if I did, the joy would be gone as well. So I take the memories as they come, accepting them all, letting them guide me whenever I can." — Nicholas Sparks, *Dear John*

Running from things that make us sad or feel painful is the least effective way to make those feelings go away, and if you don't deal with them, they tend to cast a shadow during happy moments.

Reflection: What are some ways to deal with painful memories?

DAY 150:

"You cannot pursue all your goals simultaneously or satisfy all your desires at once. And it's an emotional drain to think you can. Instead, you must focus on long-term fulfillment rather than short-term success and, at various points in your life, think carefully about your priorities."
— Eric C. Sinoway

It is hard to reach your goals if you haven't prioritized them. Try to reach several of them at once and you can get overwhelmed, feel stuck and unable to choose what to work on next then give up altogether. Gathering your thoughts and remembering why you created your goals in the first place can be an effective starting position. Remembering those reasons energizes you and helps you get started again.

If you get bored quickly and need a change of pace to keep you going, it is helpful to make a list of the three or four major things you would like to accomplish in a day and about how much time you want to devote to each project. So one thing might get two hours, another gets one hour and another thirty minutes. Then set a timer, so you are only concentrating on that one thing for thirty minutes at a time. Take a break and walk around, get something to drink, whatever you need to do as long as it is only a few minutes (it can be helpful to time breaks also) then either switch tasks for the next thirty minutes or go back to your original task. You can focus on most things for at least thirty minutes, but after that attention can wane and trying to push on is counterproductive.

Reflection: Do you think breaking down goals into smaller steps is a strategy that would work for you?

DAY 151:

"The major work of the world is not done by geniuses. It is done by ordinary people, with balance in their lives, who have learned to work in an extraordinary manner." — Gordon B. Hinckley

I've always been surprised to look around and see in both big places and small that the majority of the work accomplished often seems to be done by a relatively tiny group of people. People that seem to have a lot on their plate, but like a healthy meal, it all balances out. These ordinary people have discovered that in balancing their lives, they find the energy to keep going and the energy to make a real difference.

Reflection: If your life was like a well-balanced diet, what portions would you give to different activities to keep yourself healthy and full of energy?

DAY 152:

"Balance. It was all about balance. That had been one of the first things that she had learned: the center of the seesaw has neither up nor down, but upness and downness flow through it while it remains unmoved. You had to be the center of the seesaw, so the pain flowed through you, not into you. It was very hard. But she could do it!" — Terry Pratchett, I Shall Wear Midnight

It's crucial to have things that center and balance your life, so that when things get out of kilter, and you have a bad day, a bad week, or even a bad year, you realize that doesn't make for a bad life. What is happening in this moment, no matter how good or how painful it might be, will eventually pass. However, your core character lasts and helps you make it through to keep steady until things change again.

Reflection: What do you think are some things that keep a person centered so they can handle the ups and downs of life?

DAY 153:

"I want to caution you against the idea that balance has to be a routine that looks the same week in and week out."
— Kevin Thoman

There is a difference between having a structure to your life and being in balance. Structure helps you to stay organized and provides a framework for the systems of your life, but balance can be about both the need for structure and the need for release from a structure. You need a little of both to feel balanced. This need for balance is why students get excited about summer vacation but often find they get bored and look forward to being back into the routine of the school year.

Reflection: Can you think of a time in your life when having too much structure or too much free time left your life feeling unbalanced?

DAY 154:

"When Coleridge tried to define beauty, he returned always to one deep thought; beauty, he said, is unity in variety! Science is nothing else than the search to discover unity in the wild variety of nature,—or, more exactly, in the variety of our experience. Poetry, painting, the arts are the same search, in Coleridge's phrase, for unity in variety."
— Bronowski

Creating a life of beauty is about finding the unity in variety, a poetic way of saying it is all about balance. For me, I often become extremely unbalanced before I realize I need to readjust myself. Hours of overtime work can lead to a complete break in which I suddenly find myself watching five movies back to back to completely disengage my mind from thoughts of what seems like never-ending work that needs to be completed.

At those times, it is helpful for me to remember that balance happens differently for everyone. When I think about nature I see this also happens, hot summer droughts followed by torrential downpours with no end in sight. It's o.k., unity in variety, balance among unbalanced forces. It is realizing the need for change that is the key to seeking balance.

Reflection: Have you ever felt yourself being extremely unbalanced? What were some things that helped you balance yourself?

DAY 155:

"Never ask the tight-rope walker how he keeps his balance.
if he stops to think about it, he falls off."
— Terry Pratchett, A Hat Full of Sky

There may be times in your life when nothing makes
sense, and the easiest way to keep balance is just to keep
walking forward. Do what feels like the next right thing.
You may be surprised about how the next step brings you
to a new destination, perspective, or hope.

Reflection: If you have created good systems in your life,
frustrating forces won't have as big an impact on your life,
you just deal with things and move on. What is a system
that you have around you that has helped you maintain
balance during a difficult time?

DAY 156:

"There seems to be a sense of balance or equilibrium that nature attempts to achieve with the usage of cycles, leading us to the concept of self-organization and spontaneous order."
— Kat Lahr, Parallelism Of Cyclicality

Hiking in the forest, you might feel like nature is a wild and chaotic beast, but when you look closer, you are amazed at all the structures and cycles that surround everything from weather patterns to hibernating bears. Everything seems to have some type of system and organized thought behind it. The lessons we can take from this are many and deserve our time to explore them. Just like a wheel, balance is often a circle or cycle that keeps everything moving along.

Reflection: What lessons can you learn from nature that would help you keep a balanced life?

DAY 157:

"Balance is not a passive resting place—it takes work, balancing the giving and the taking, the raking out and the putting in."
— Robin Wall Kimmerer, *Braiding Sweetgrass: Indigenous Wisdom, Scientific Knowledge, and the Teachings of Plants*

The balance of the work/rest cycle may seem like complete opposites, but it is a very active process. Even when we go to sleep, we find that our minds stay awake, telling us stories of the past or the future, or entertaining us with fanciful tales that we repeat to our friends the next day.

Reflection: Why do you think our minds are still active even when we are sleeping?

DAY 158:

One of my favorite games is a math card came called "24". The goal of the game is to use the four numbers given on the card and see if you can find a way by adding, subtracting, multiplying, or dividing to use all four of the digits only one time to get to the answer twenty-four.

When I first started playing this game, I found it frustrating because I didn't think I was very good at math. The more I played it, the easier it became, and I found I was quickly getting the answers. It was a huge shift for me to let go of my preconceived notion that I just wasn't capable of doing math quickly in my head.

To help maintain balance it helps to look at the beliefs that we have that limit us and examine if they are always true. If we can find times when they are not true, then we know we have a limiting belief that is holding us back in life. Limiting beliefs can create fear and anxiety in our lives when there is no reason for it to be there.

Reflection: Can you think of a limiting belief you or someone else might have that could cause anxiety? How could building on the things you do know about that subject help to lower the stress?

DAY 159:

"Happiness is like a butterfly, the more you chase it, the more it will elude you, but if you turn your attention to other things, it will come and sit softly on your shoulder." - quote usually attributed to Henry David Thoreau

The other thing I like about the math game "24" is that it helps me remember that there can be many ways to get a satisfactory solution to a problem. When I let go of my need to find one specific way to find a solution to an issue it can be very freeing.

Sometimes I just say, "If I wanted to....what are some ways that could happen?" Then I think of a few ways or some action steps I could start taking, and then I let it go and turn my attention to other things. Letting go, keeping my mind in a happy place, and trusting that a way will present itself almost seems too easy, but it seems to work most of the time. Sometimes the answer presents itself almost immediately, and sometimes it takes years, but it usually works out.

Setting goals is about finding a solution you would like to reach and then finding a way to reach that solution. Letting go of the need to only have one way to do that can open up a lot of doors and fun along the way.

Reflection: Do you think letting go and keeping your mind in a happy emotional state will help you reach your goals faster? Why?

DAY 160:

"By choosing to have a calm response to what seems negative you bring clarity and balance to your message."
— Bryant McGill

It seems to be true that what you resists, persists. When you choose to focus on the parts of any situation that are good, even if they are problematic, finding a solution always seems to happen faster and easier.

When discussing any situation or working through a problem, keeping a level, balanced thought process will help you work through it quicker and easier.

Reflection: What are things that will help you to develop a habit of calm and positive thinking so you can handle it when adverse situations enter your life?

DAY 161:

"Sometimes a pat on the back or just a simple word of comfort is all that it takes to bring someone under heavy stress back to balance." — JA Perez

"You are safe."
"You can do this."
"Everything is going to be o.k."
"Breathe."
"You are capable."
"You can handle this."
"I'm here for you."
"This is tough, but I believe in you."
"It's o.k. to cry, it's o.k. to let go."
"You can get through this."
"This is manageable, break it into small steps and you can do it."
"Just take one step at a time."
"I appreciate you."
"You have put a lot of effort into this, it shows."
"Hugs!"

Reflection: What are some words that have been said to you at just the right time that have made a difference in helping you rebalance?

DAY 162:
"What is joy without sorrow? What is success without failure? What is a win without a loss? What is health without illness? You have to experience each if you are to appreciate the other. There is always going to be suffering. it's how you look at your suffering, how you deal with it, that will define you." -Mark Twain

Mark Twain is the well-known author of many books and short stories including The Adventures of Tom Sawyer. What is not known as well-known about Mark Twain is that while he could be considered the first stand-up comedian, traveling from place to place to give humorous speeches, the reason he did that was because he was raising money to pay off debts he incurred from a bad investment. Following the ups and downs of his life is like watching a ping pong ball bounce across the floor. It included great success and adventure as well as great sorrow and moments of uncertainty.

A visit to his hometown of Hannibal, Missouri will convince anyone that Twain was defined by his ability to make good of whatever life handed him, and to share that good with others. Many of the jobs in Hannibal surround a tourism industry built up around the life of Mark Twain. People loved him for his willingness to approach the ups and downs of life with a sense of grace and forward movement. He never sugar-coated life. Instead, his sense of humor helped people think about difficult topics in a different way.

Reflection: When you think about the ways you encounter the ups and downs of life, what are some words that would define you? Are there other words you would like to represent you in the future?

DAY 163:

"When the world follows the Tao, horses run free to fertilize the fields. When the world does not follow the Tao, warhorses are bred outside the cities." Tao Te Ching Chapter 46, translated by J H McDonald

We live in a world that has not taken the idea of balance and ecology as seriously as it could have. Things are changing, and in some places changing rapidly, but there is still a lot to be accomplished to return our planet to a place of ecological balance. A place where clean water, clean air, and sustainable building practices for everyone are all the expected norm. A place where the value of creating a sustainable future is more important than making quick money to benefit just a few people in the present moment. It isn't an impossible goal, it just starts with the decision that it must be done. A shift in values creates the momentum from what is, to what is possible.

Reflection: What are some things that you think would make our world more ecologically balanced? What are some ways those things could be accomplished? What is one thing you could do to make a difference?

DAY 164:

"We find our energies are actually cramped when we are overanxious to succeed." Michel de Montaigne

There is something remarkably freeing about seeking to do well on anything in life and yet letting go of the need to succeed. Finding the balance that allows creating, learning, and doing, while still being fully aware that you are enough just as you are, is a place of joy enabling you to do more than you ever dreamed. When we become anxious that we have to be the best, we sometimes shut down our happiness and ability to go beyond what seems possible for us to accomplish.

Reflection: If you are over anxious to succeed and not in a place of joy and self-compassion when you are working on a project what are some ways you could improve your mindset and emotions?

DAY 165:
"Haters' don't hate you, they hate self and project the energy outward because there is no courage to confront internal fears. Therefore, ignore hate or else it becomes you, also." — T.F. Hodge

When dealing with someone that seems to create drama around them no matter what the circumstance, it may be that they have a lot of internal issues they don't want to face. Their ability to attract craziness into their lives can be directly proportional to their desire not to deal with their inner emotions and disappointments. Unfortunately, their tornado of craziness can suck you in with an unbelievably quick force that may seem to come out of nowhere.

So how do you deal with these crazy makers? The biggest shelter in this storm is really thinking through what things need attention and what doesn't. If their endless chatter sucks you in, find a way to politely change the conversation or even physically walk away from them. If there are things you can control, take care of them, but don't give a lot of emotional energy to the things you can't control. Focus on other areas of your life. The reality is that most likely this too will pass if you give it less attention. The crazy maker gets bored and moves on to something else that will meet their emotional need to escape their real issues.

Reflection: How someone else feels about you is not really under your control, how you treat them is. Think of someone you might have difficulty with, do you find that you think about them too much? Sending positive thoughts and moving on might be your best option.

DAY 166:

Part of living a deliberate, successfully balanced life has to do with your own determination of what that looks like for you. No one else can define success for you because no one else really understands what success means to you. Your definition of success is a brilliant blend of all the intense experiences you alone have experienced. Balance and success might look entirely different to you than it does to the person sitting next to you.

Reflection: What is your definition of what balance and success look like?

DAY 167:

One of my students recently learned how to roller skate. He shared with me the secret to success in keeping your balance is to lean forward. I realized as soon as he said it that this applies to life in general. To maintain a healthy balance, it is sometimes helpful to lean forward or to think about what is going to be on in your schedule in the future.

If you can anticipate what things will need your time and attention, it is easier to find a structure that will help you maintain balance. Your needs will change based on many things coming up in the future, including changing schools, getting a new job, your family structure, even the upcoming weather. Realizing that things change, helps you lean forward to make any adjustments today that need to be made so it is easier to keep your balance when those changes occur.

Reflection: What big or small things do you foresee happening in the next week, month, or year that you might need to take into account to keep your life in balance?

DAY 168:

Playing the "What if?" game might be a good way to interpret what type of lifestyle will bring you a sense of balance. "What if I went to an Ivy League college?" "What if I got into the high school of my choice?" "What if that coach noticed how great I am at basketball?" "What if I didn't get into the high school of my choice?" "What if I don't ever get chosen for student council?" "What if I decide I'm o.k. regardless of what happens in my life?"

When you seriously consider what it would be like to reach your highest heights or your lowest lows, it might surprise you. What might seem to be the epitome of success or failure may actually lose its power. You realize that reaching that point won't really define you as much as you think it does. You may start to understand that you are defined more by your character and how you approach life than what actually happens to you in life.

Reflection: There are a lot of lessons to be learned in life whether we are at our absolute peak of success or in the depths of despair. What are some lessons that you can learn from both a perceived success and from a perceived failure?

DAY 169:

"The simplification of life is one of the steps to inner peace. A persistent simplification will create an inner and outer well-being that places harmony in one's life."-Peace Pilgrim

When our life is over-cluttered and over-booked, there is no margin for peace; our lives quickly become unbalanced. The trick is to subtract from our lives rather than add. How do we slow down, how do we create time for meaningful lives versus just busy lives? It takes time and energy to look at the things that have collected around us and really question their value, letting go of them if we need to.

Reflection: Would simplifying and creating more margin in your life change anything? What would you start with first?

DAY 170:
"Nobody can bring you peace but yourself." -Ralph Waldo Emerson

There have been many times in life when I've realized my stress was completely self-created. I've imagined that the people around me would be disappointed or angry with me if I didn't match up to a particular standard I've believed they had for me, only to discover later that they were never holding me to that standard. Other times there have been standards people have held me to that with reflection I realized I didn't agree with their opinions or have any desire to meet the standard they were setting.

Reflection: Why is finding peace something you can do only for yourself?

DAY 171:

Sometimes balance can be a struggle because you have a hard time transitioning from one activity to another. If that is the case, creating habits that naturally lead from one activity to another may be helpful. For instance, if you know you need to leave your house at a certain time every morning it may help to put on specific music that gets you energized and going but lasts only a certain amount of time so you know when the song is over, you need to be out the door.

Reflection: Think about areas where you feel like your time is eaten up or you have a difficult time transitioning into another activity. What are some ways that you could ease the transition so you can maintain balance and margin in your life?

DAY 172:

A big part of being an Everyday Hero is choosing what you believe is right or wrong and living that out. It seems like it would be a simple endeavor, treat others as you would want to be treated is a golden rule across many religions, but, in reality, it can be tough and things don't always fall into manageable categories. A lot of the moral dilemmas you will face will be very complicated. Choosing to think about your core values in advance will help you stay balanced when confronted with difficult choices.

Reflection: What are some ways you determine what is morally right and wrong in your life?

DAY 173:

"I hope you live a life you are proud of. If you find that you are not, I hope you have the strength to start all over again." -F. Scott Fitzgerald

One of the beautiful things about life is that not only do you have the ability to learn from your mistakes, but you can start fresh with new knowledge of what didn't work. Facing consequences can be tough, but how you face them can make all the difference in how your life proceeds.

Reflection: Is there anything in your life you would change if you had a time machine? What things could you change now or have you already done that would transform that experience from something negative to something positive?

DAY 174:

"As is a tale, so is life: not how long it is, but how good it is, is what matters." -Lucius Annaeus Seneca

We don't have any real choice over how long our life will be, but we do have a lot of options that will determine how good our life can be. Creating a life that feels good from the inside out is a matter of choosing our attitudes and actions.

Reflection: Most of life is not a matter of what happens to us but how we respond to what happens to us. What are the consistent responses you can choose that will help your life be one you consider, "good"?

DAY 175:

"Courage is fire, and bullying is smoke."
Benjamin Disraeli

Bullying is sometimes very subtle, and often the bully doesn't even realize the damage they are doing, most frequently those that stand by and say nothing don't understand the damage they are doing. If you are astute enough to realize you are being bullied or someone around you is being bullied, it can take real courage to stand up for what is right. That type of courage realizes this moment is not your whole life, but it might be someone else's.

Reflection: If you don't have the courage to stand up to someone that is being a bully what other things could you do to help the situation or how could you increase your courage so you can make a difference?

DAY 176:

"Culture makes people understand each other better. And if they understand each other better in their soul, it is easier to overcome the economic and political barriers. But first they have to understand that their neighbor is, in the end, just like them, with the same problems, the same questions." -Paulo Coelho

When you think about the eternal questions in life about meaning, love, and purpose, what you are really asking is, "How do I proceed?" The answer often comes back as, "One step at a time." As you journey forth as an everyday hero, there will be many times that the future seems too impossible and your goals unachievable, but moving forward with faith in yourself and faith in the process will allow you to go further than you have ever dreamed.

Reflection: What are some of the universal questions that most people wonder about regardless of their background? How can we work together to help answer those questions?

DAY 177:

"Step with care and great tact, and remember that life's a great balancing act." -Dr. Seuss

Dr. Seuss is the well-loved author of children's books, but many of those books might never have been written if Dr. Seuss hadn't run into an old friend on the very day he was planning on burning the manuscript of his first children's book, *And to Think I Saw it on Mulberry Street.* The manuscript had already been rejected by over twenty publishers, but the chance encounter led to the book's publication by Vanguard Press.

Later Houghton Mifflin publishers commissioned Dr. Seuss to create a children's book that included 250 of the most common used sight words for new readers. This commission led to the creation of one of his most famous books, *The Cat in the Hat.*

Reflection: Life is often about balancing: when to continue and when to let go, what are some ways to know when to do either one?

DAY 178:

"The world has the habit of making room for the man whose actions show that he knows where he is going." Napoleon Hill

Sometimes the direction of your dreams is very clear, you know just what to do, and other times your dreams feel so foggy you aren't even sure there is a road much less what you need to find it. Don't get discouraged. Keep sorting through your feelings and find the things that bring you joy. Those things are your guideposts helping you find where you need to be.

Reflection: If you don't know what direction you want to go to in life, ask yourself these questions and let your intuition and time help you find the way:

1.   What would the answer be if I did know?
2.   What would it take to create a life I enjoy in the next six months or year? Five years? Ten years?

DAY 179:

"As a single footstep will not make a path on the earth, so a single thought will not make a pathway in the mind. To make a deep physical path, we walk again and again. To make a deep mental path, we must think over and over the kind of thoughts we wish to dominate our lives."
Henry David Thoreau

Maintaining balance and creating a life we are proud of are the main tasks of an everyday hero. It happens thought by thought, choice by choice, step by step. Over and over until the life we live is not the trail ahead of us but the trail we have left for others to follow.

Reflection: When you look back over the past year what are the memories that you are the most proud of? That stand out the most? The ones you return to over and over? Do those moments seem to point towards the direction of your future? What things would you like to change? What would you keep the same?

DAY 180:

Have you ever been on a see-saw? It is a great example of how balance works. One side goes up as the other goes down, but it is the spot in the middle that keeps everything balanced. Picture time as a see-saw, you can think of one side being the past and one side being the future, but the balance is found in the present moment. It can be easy to spend too much time at either end, feeling nostalgic for the past or lost in dreams of a perfect future. There is nothing wrong with being on either of those ends, as long as you don't stay there. It is in the present moment where your choices are being made, the choices that lead you to a better future and eventually give you a past worth looking back on with pride.

Reflection: As you journey forward remember that being an Everyday Hero is about the choices and actions you make today with the options you have right in front of you. What are some things you have learned during this journey that are influencing today and providing a different way of looking at tomorrow?

ABOUT THE AUTHOR

Peggy E. Pate-Smith grew up in a small town in Texas where her favorite place to read a book was on her front porch, occasionally stopping to watch the sheep in the pasture across the road. She left that porch to get her bachelor's degree from A.C.U. her Masters of Montessori Education from Endicott College, and to do both Elementary and Middle School Montessori Teacher Training at the Houston Montessori Center in Houston, Texas.

This is her fourth book. Other titles include a travel book, *Reading 10,000 Books: A Journey of Body and Soul,* *Implications for Peace: Montessori Elementary Education,* and a middle school fiction book: *Peaceful Farm Montessori.*

She continues to love to read, enjoys traveling, writing books, and flying kites. Her favorite fairytale as a child was, *The Elves and the Shoemaker.*

www.ingramcontent.com/pod-product-compliance
Lightning Source LLC
Chambersburg PA
CBHW060751050426
42449CB00008B/1357